LIFE after BELSEN

A first-hand account of the survivors of Bergen-Belsen and other horror camps in Europe after World War II.

Simon Bloomberg (CBE)

with Al Gibson

About the Author
Simon Bloomberg

Simon Bloomberg (1894-1981) was a Jewish humanitarian best known for his historic role in resettling the displaced persons of Europe after World War II. He was awarded a CBE for a life of service to the British Colonial Office and recognised by the United Nations for the vital part he played in relieving the suffering and saving lives of victims of war. The Jewish Committee for Relief Abroad also commended him for his devotion towards helping survivors of Nazi persecution to rebuild their lives.

German historians, Angelika Konigseder and Juliane Wetzel wrote about Simon in their book *Waiting for Hope: Jewish Displaced Persons in Post-World War II Germany.* "Bloomberg knew the official mind and could talk on equal terms with the military and civil authorities. There was soon a different atmosphere at Belsen."

Historic documents relating to Simon's time at Bergen-Belsen (Hohne) are housed in The Wiener Library for the study of the Holocaust and Genocide, in London. For more about Simon Bloomberg visit www.simonbloomberg.com.

At the end of World War II Europe overflowed with Displaced People (DPs). The horror camps of the Nazis did not close straight after liberation. The people of the camps had to wait to be resettled and it was Jewish survivors who waited the longest.

Simon Bloomberg provides a candid, though often humorous, eye-witness account of what took place in the DP camps after the war, including the one at Bergen-Belsen that he led from 1946 to 1947. This camp only closed in 1951 after its people had finally emigrated to Israel to start a new life.

About the Editor
Al Gibson

Al Gibson has worked in mass media for some thirty years, in the UK, USA, Israel and South Africa. He has a Bachelor of Journalism degree and has served as a journalist, publisher, communications officer, copywriter and editor. He is also an internationally published author. Al ran a publishing company in South Africa for ten years and has lived in England since 2001, where he works for a global television network. He has interviewed many inspirational leaders during the course of his career and as a writer aims to capture real-life accounts of people who have overcome major obstacles.

Biographies Al has written include *Life on the Line* the biography of Des Sinclair and *Mother of Malawi* the life story of Annie Chikhwaza. Al met Simon Bloomberg's daughter Eva Spiers through a mutual friend, Pat Poole and was given a collection of seventy-year-old diaries, reams of aging typed pages of an initial manuscript and a batch of faded handwritten letters. After a lengthy editing process, *Life After Belsen* is the result. For more information about Al Gibson visit his website at www.algibsonauthor.com.

Dedication

Dedicated to
the displaced people of Europe
after World War II
and to all those who wait in hope
to be resettled into a place
they can call home.

Simon Bloomberg

Simon Bloomberg (1894-1981)

Life After Belsen by Simon Bloomberg
Copyright © 2017 Eva Spiers
The right of Eva Spiers to be identified as the author of this work has been asserted in accordance with the Copyright, Designs and Patents Act 1988.
All rights reserved.

No part of this publication may be reproduced or transmitted in any form or by any means, electronic or mechanical, including photocopy, recording, or any information storage and retrieval system, without permission in writing from the publisher.

Published by: Al Gibson
E-mail: al@algibsonauthor.com

First Edition, UK 2.11.2017
Rest of the World 27.1.2018
ISBN-13: 9781976112973 / ISBN-10: 1976112974

ACKNOWLEDGMENTS
The Wiener Library for the Study of the Holocaust and Genocide, London.
Pat Poole, Jamie Spiers, Charlie Cluff
Mark Bloomberg and Sandra Shaw

Project visionary, interviews and final edit: Eva Spiers
Documentation and family tree: Norah Bloomberg
Research, editing and design: Al Gibson

A catalogue record for this book is available from the British Library.

Contents

Foreword:	**An Unsung Hero** by Eva Spiers	9
1:	**A Tragic Search for Survivors**	
	Auschwitz to Bergen-Belsen	13
2:	**My Jewish Heritage**	
	The Cohen Connection	19
3:	**The Civil Service**	
	London & Liverpool	31
4:	**World War I**	
	France & Flanders	41
5:	**Chasing the Sun**	
	Kenya & Jamaica	47
6:	**An Opportunity for Something Worthwhile**	57
7:	**Serving the United Nations**	
	France, Belgium & Holland	65
8:	**Aftermath of World War II**	
	Deutschland	77
9:	**The Polish & Ukrainian Camps**	
	Salzgitter, Germany	97
10:	**Microcosm of the Hunted**	
	Polish Repatriation	113
11:	**The Last Jew of Peine**	
	Adelheide & Peine Camps, Germany	123

12:	**The Führer's Followers**	
	A Glimpse into their Minds	135
Photographs		145
13	**My Own People the Jews**	
	Bergen-Belsen	153
14:	**Life at Belsen**	
	Surviving the DP Camp	169
15:	**Let My People Go**	
	Eretz Yisrael	181
16:	**Back to Belsen**	
	Jewish Committee for Relief Abroad	193
17:	**In Search of a Normal Life**	
	Kaunitz Camp, Germany	201
18:	**Other Jewish DP Camps**	
	The American Zone	207
19:	**A New Jewish Refugee Crisis**	
	Vienna, Austria	217
20:	**Back Behind Barbed Wire**	
	The Exodus	231
Afterword:	**A Life of Service** by Al Gibson	
	Bloomberg, a Brief Biography	249
Appendix		267

Foreword

An Unsung Hero
by Eva Spiers

My father, Simon Bloomberg was one of Great Britain's unsung heroes. He was a clever man, a generous person who was most forgiving and loved by everyone. He served in the British Army in World War I, in the Colonial Service during World War II, and devoted his life to serving the people of the Commonwealth. He is best known for his tireless work amongst displaced people in Europe from 1945 to 1948, including his own people, the Jews.

He considered it a privilege to bring hope into the desperate lives of thousands who had lost their homes, their family members and for some, the very will to live. While

Life After Belsen

many of these unfortunate souls were Jewish it wasn't just Jews he helped. He assisted many Poles, Ukrainians, Hungarians, and others and helped those who had survived the Holocaust recover from the horrors of the Nazi regime.

Though honoured by King George VI with a CBE and recognised by the Jewish Committee for Relief Abroad his extraordinary contribution towards resettling homeless people across Europe has never been documented publicly nor have his deep insights into post-war Europe been made known, despite the fact that he was a prolific writer.

'Pop' sent hundreds of letters to us from towns and cities across Europe and I encouraged him to share his experiences more widely. He wrote this book in the 1970s, but sadly it never made the bookshelves while he was alive. But now as we remember the centenary of the Balfour Declaration of 1917 and move towards the Seventy-Fifth Anniversary of the End of the Holocaust, in 2020, I'm delighted his story is finally published. My thanks to Al Gibson for making sense of my dad's manuscript and framing it in a context that is still relevant for today. I feel I have been given a gift from God because I never thought it was possible to encapsulate my father's story in such a dynamic way and I am extremely grateful for what this book achieves.

For me, it provides a remarkable historical record that challenges prejudice and refutes those who deny the horrors of the past so they aren't repeated. It also instills such hope for the future, that no matter how displaced we may be, there is a place for each one of us, that we can call home, and where we can be the best possible neighbours to those next door as well as to those who are homeless.

> *"For me, Life After Belsen provides a remarkable historical record that challenges prejudice, refutes those who deny past horrors, and instills such hope that no matter how displaced we may be, there is a home waiting for us."*

I had to do something with the documents that my sister so carefully collected, all the seventy-year-old dairies my father so dutifully wrote, the hundreds of handwritten letters he penned to my mother, overflowing with love and his reams of typed pages filled with nuggets of wisdom, wit, and breadth of view. Now you hold them in your hand, judiciously compiled into a readable format that will inspire you, whether you're interested in history or not, whether you're Jewish or not and whether you're an up and coming reader like my grandchildren or share my vintage. Now in my eighties myself, as I look back on all my father accomplished I realise how important it is to leave a legacy to coming generations to challenge them in

Life After Belsen

the years that lie ahead. In a world where tragically people are still displaced and refugees are more numerous than ever, my father's example is a timeless reminder to forsake racism, persecution, and genocide and be a better neighbour wherever we find ourselves.

Like Pop who served in different parts of the world, East Africa, Europe and the West Indies, his children, grandchildren and great grandchildren now live on different continents. The families he helped resettle can also be found in an A to Z of nations. I don't know their names, many of them will have passed on by now, but I still hope to hear from their families. I am glad my family was able to contribute towards bringing some light during a time of great darkness. What follows is my father's story that shows how we can make a difference despite the obstacles that face us.

> *"To all who mourn in Israel, He will give a crown of beauty for ashes, a joyous blessing instead of mourning, festive praise instead of despair. In their righteousness, they will be like great oaks that the Lord has planted." (Isaiah 61:3)*

Dr Eva (Bloomberg) Spiers (PhD)
Brisbane, Australia, 2017

Chapter 1
A Tragic Search for Survivors
Auschwitz to Bergen-Belsen

The very first time I encountered Jewish survivors of the Holocaust was in August 1945. While returning to my base at Salzgitter, Germany from a visit to a camp for displaced persons, I passed a forlorn-looking group of stragglers. They were limping along the main highway towards Brunswick. This was not an unusual sight at the time, particularly in this part of Germany, where the whole population seemed to be on the hike. Everywhere one went there were scores of demobbed soldiers and civilians streaming out of the Russian Zone just a few miles away. There was also a constant stream of displaced persons of all nationalities on the move – north,

Life After Belsen

south and west – any direction away from the east where relations with our Russian allies were deteriorating day by day and the Iron Curtain was starting to descend.

There was something about this group of stragglers that impelled me to stop the Bedford truck and take another look. It was the menfolk of the group that arrested my attention. They were bearded, like their counterparts in the East End of London, that I'd seen in Whitechapel on a Saturday morning. I had to make sure so I pulled into the kerb, walked up to the group and addressed them in Yiddish of which I remembered a little.

> *"They had come from Auschwitz and were going to Belsen. The group was not related, just camp brothers and sisters, banded together to search for relatives who may have escaped extermination."*

"Rist Yidden?" (Are you Jews?) I asked. They looked at my British service uniform without replying, until I added, again in Yiddish, "I am an English Jew." Then the storm broke. They all spoke together, far too fast for me to understand, and when the initial excitement had subsided, I asked the woman who appeared to be the mother of the group, to speak slowly and tell me who they were and where they were going.

Simon Bloomberg

They had come from Auschwitz and were going to Belsen. They were a group of eleven, four men, five women and two young children who they had picked up, she said, on the way, from German people who had hidden them in their homes during the troubled years.

The members of the group were not related, just camp brothers and sisters, banded together in a search for relatives who might have escaped extermination and who may still be alive in one of the liberated camps. This tragic search for survivors of the gas chambers and incinerators was to continue for years but, for the majority, it was to be a search in vain. As if to establish their bona fides they showed me the numbers tattooed on their arms, prefixed by the letter 'A' for Auschwitz, the sadistic method of registration that only Nazi devils could devise.

They were clothed in rags, the women in blouses crudely made from hessian bags and make shift slacks, and the men in tattered oddments of clothing, and all the adults had felting on their feet for shoes. It was impossible to guess the ages of the adults because of their bedraggled appearance. The two children though were well clothed.

Their destination troubled me because I had heard and read that the horror camp at Bergen-Belsen had been destroyed and the survivors removed but my newly found kinsfolk were certain that there were still thousands of Jews at Belsen.

Life After Belsen

After a long discussion in which my limited German and worse Yiddish were taxed to the utmost, I managed to explain that I worked for the United Nations. I finally convinced them that in accordance with the functions of the United Nations Relief and Rehabilitation Administration (UNRRA) it was my job to help them on their way and could probably help find them transport for the rest of their journey. So they eventually agreed to come with me to an adjacent DP camp on the Goslar Brunswick Road.

It was a camp for the recalcitrant Poles, the 'hard cases' who wouldn't adhere to camp rules and regulations, and were forever in trouble with the military police. The Polish camp leader wasn't overly welcoming of the new arrivals but when he saw their condition and that they had not so much as a suitcase between them, he allotted them a hut near the guardroom where the camp police could protect them by keeping intruders away.

They were given bowls of soup, loaves of rye bread, and beds for the night, mattresses filled with straw. To assure them, I promised to return in a couple of hours with a few supplies from our UNRRA store, where fortunately we had recently received some POW Red Cross parcels, and I returned with two of these.

I felt a bit like Joseph when he was giving corn to his brothers in Egypt. The group had long forgotten what decent food looked like and could not believe that this generous gift was gratis and for nothing. The children had never seen chocolate and could not be persuaded to even taste it. For the adults, the cigarettes were a treasure trove more important than the food, which is understandable to a tobacco starved-addict, but they seemed to grasp their value for barter.

> *"I felt a bit like Joseph when he was giving corn to his brothers in Egypt. The group had long forgotten what decent food looked like and could not believe that this was gratis and for nothing."*

The following day was a Friday, and I arranged to have them transported from the camp to our assembly centre in Salzgitter where we had a small reserve of clothing and footwear kept for transit displaced persons. I turned them loose in what to them must have felt like being in Aladdin's cave, to choose new garments for themselves. Then, hot baths were prepared for them and when they reappeared the transformation was quite unbelievable. The unkempt, bedraggled nomads had, as if by the touch of a magic wand, been changed into a party of neatly dressed young people. Whereas before they had looked old, they now looked young and relaxed.

A bigger surprise was to follow for them on Friday

Life After Belsen

evening as the Jewish Sabbath began, and I had told the caterer, a chatty German hausfrau, to arrange a meal for eleven people, guests of mine, two of them children. The guests were invited to arrange themselves at table in order of age, because the senior was to light the traditional candles and say the blessing preceding the evening meal. I thought that I was case hardened by now but that memorable Sabbath meal was almost too much for my emotions.

After a day's rest, the party left in the charge of an American welfare officer, who when she returned told me of the new Belsen, a huge Panzer barracks, two miles or so away from the old horror camp, where there were thousands of Jews and Poles, most of them survivors of the infamous concentration camp. The military leaders in charge of the camp used its correct name, 'Hohne', but to those Jews who had survived the Holocaust it would never be anything but Belsen. Little did I know then that I would become the UNRRA director of the camp and working with displaced people would become my greatest life calling. It seemed everything in my life led up to this point.

Chapter 2
My Jewish Heritage
The Cohen Connection

Cohen was my family's original surname, but like many Jewish families it was changed to fit in with those who couldn't do without our skills, yet found it hard to be associated with our faith or culture. The irony of course is that Bloomberg became a well-known Jewish surname! It was the name I was always proud to bear and throughout my life I held the cause of the Jewish people greatly in my heart.

Perhaps this deep connection goes back as far as my maternal grandmother who was the only grandparent I ever knew. She was a diminutive figure in a traditional black dress, who would sit in an armchair alongside the kitchen fire at

Life After Belsen

our home in Liverpool. Despite her apparent great age, and to me as a youngster of ten, she was very, very old, her hair was jet black and her cherub-like face had few wrinkles. Her arrival always brought a hive of culinary activity, she was an excellent cook, made superb jams and other dainties that made her popular with her grandchildren.

'Bubby' as we called her was born in Stettin (Szczecin) in Poland on the Baltic Coast in the 1840s. She had come to England as a young girl, where she'd met my grandfather, a Jewish immigrant of some years her senior. He had been born near Moscow, the son of reasonably well-off parents who had sent him to Great Britain to escape military service in Russia. War, however, had caught up with him and according to family history he served with the British forces in the Crimean War as an interpreter.

Upon his return, he and my bubbe (Yiddish for grandma) married and they settled in South Wales, where like many of his kinsmen, my grandfather took to selling jewellery from door to door in the mining towns of the Rhondda Valley. During one of his journeys he called in at a wedding party to show his wares, was invited in and partook of generous amounts of strong liquor with disastrous consequences. My granny always maintained that he never really recovered from this bout for he died shortly afterwards.

Left with five young children and little money she decided to go to Russia to her late husband's parents and see what help she could raise. To strengthen her case, and as evidence of her plight, she took along with her, her eldest boy and eldest girl, my mother, Annie, then a child of about five. The long and hazardous journey across Germany, Poland and Russia left few impressions on my mother as a child, but she did recall the church bells of Moscow and riding in droshkies (horse-drawn carriages).

Financially, the quest was not a success. An offer to adopt my mother and educate her was refused and Bubby began her long trek back to Wales. It may have been as a result of this continental trip that she decided to pack up in Wales and go to Paris where she opened a gingerbread stall at the Great Exhibition, selling homemade wares to provide for her family. How long she stayed in France and why she decided to return to Wales I never found out. But, despite her long sojourn in the UK, she spoke little English. Yiddish was her mother tongue. Yiddish interspersed with German and Hebrew phrases. My knowledge of Yiddish was scant and it is to my lasting regret I never mastered the language.

In her later years, when her children had married and dispersed she made an annual circuit from South Wales to Yorkshire, then on to Lancashire visiting all her offspring but never overstaying her welcome.

On the paternal side of my family tree, my grandfather was born in Grodno, in Russian Poland, that part of the Czar's Empire where the vast majority of European Jews were settled.

Life After Belsen

He had married twice raising two families, my father Lazarus and his elder brother being the children of the first marriage. It was probably my father's inability to live peaceably with his exacting stepmother that drove him to leave Poland and go and live with an uncle in London, as soon as he could, after leaving school.

However, it was also the time of the pogroms of the 1880s that were causing so much distress for the Jewish Poles. The brutal attacks on the ghettos became more frequent and the callous indifference of the Russian Government to this savagery made the Jews realise that there was no future for them or their children in Russia. The result was an exodus probably greater in numbers than the Biblical flight from Egypt and lasting up until World War I.

"The callous indifference of the Russian Government to the pogroms made the Jews realise there was no future for them in Russia. The result was an exodus probably greater than the Biblical flight from Egypt."

A few, the idealists, went as pioneers to their ancient home in Palestine, others to friends and relatives in the more enlightened countries of Europe, but the main stream in which my grandfather and his family joined, flowed to the USA.

Simon Bloomberg

I can remember as a schoolboy seeing hundreds of these bewildered emigrants passing through the Port of Liverpool, queues of them lined up outside the offices of 'The Cunard' and 'White Star' lines, their worldly possessions restricted to the bundles they could carry, before they embarked from the Liverpool landing stage for the last lap of their journey.

Those were the days of no passport restrictions, no quotas, no Iron Curtain, none of the restrictions I would have to deal with daily after World War II. The only essentials then were the passage money and if travelling steerage, a clean bill of health. So many emigrants could be packed into the hold of one ship that the steamship companies found it a lucrative business and there was fierce competition between the shipping lines. Fares were cut so low, that at one time it was possible to cross the Atlantic for less than two pounds. My father claims to have done it for thirty shillings!

My granddad and his second family landed in New York and gravitated to the Bowery, the ghetto of the New World which seemed to absorb all the Jewish and Irish immigrants, the proverbial 'Cohens' and 'Kellys' who initially made up so large a proportion of the New York population. Grandpa had no special skills. In his hometown, he had run a liquor store, spending much of his time studying his beloved Talmud, between customers. His virtue was rewarded because he found work as a shammes (synagogue caretaker). A house went with the job and my brother and step brothers were soon

Life After Belsen

gathering the rewards of part-time employment after hours and helping with the family income. This was the pattern for immigrant youth, the paper boy to millionaire!

Grandpa must have prospered for in 1914 he had accumulated enough dollars to pay for a trip to his native Grodno, probably to tell his friends of the opportunities in the Land of the Free. Unfortunately, he arrived in Russian Poland just as World War I broke out, when the Kaiser's forces were sweeping across the country destroying everything before them. Poor grandpa was lost without trace. A photograph taken in New York, showing a bearded patriarch with strong aquiline features, a wide brow and noble head capped by the Orthodox 'yarmulke' is my only memory of him.

Meanwhile, in London, my father was pursuing an apprenticeship in the cap trade with his uncle, but it wouldn't last long. Put to work on a treadle machine sowing segments of caps for public schoolboys was not his idea of learning a trade. Hours spent in a crowded, ill-ventilated sweatshop must have disillusioned him about the joys of an escape to freedom.

His uncle had prospered, helped by his entrepreneurial son-in-law who had taken over the management of the business. The factory was on the ground floor of a large Victorian house in Spitalfields, above which the family lived. My father, the poor relation, was given board and lodging; a pittance of pocket money; and was treated as any other apprentice. His cousins, English born, had social aspirations and the presence of a Yiddish-speaking relation, full of the revolutionary ideas of young Russians of that era, rather cramped their style.

Meanwhile, my mother found herself in Leeds. She had little formal education. Bubby's roving had prevented regular schooling but my mother had a bright intelligence and a retentive memory that enabled her to learn quickly and make the most of her limited opportunities. At the age of fifteen she auditioned for a pantomime showing at the Leeds Music Hall where she was trained to dance and sing. For a whole season, she appeared in the front row of the chorus line, loving every moment of it. She wanted to carry on with a stage career, but Bubby's abhorrence to the theatre was to be a stumbling block.

It was at this fortuitous moment that my father appeared on the scene as a possible suitor, an earnest young man who claimed social status by reference to his rich uncle in London. After his hoped-for bride had been scrutinised by his London relations, where she passed with flying colours, my father returned to Leeds, the answer to Bubby's prayer and they were married, he a bridegroom of nineteen and she a couple of years younger.

The first years of their marriage must have been hectic for they quickly relocated to Edinburgh. They had my elder sister there but soon moved again to Liverpool where a year

Life After Belsen

later, in 1894 I first saw the light of day. Before another year was out my father, taking advantage of the cheap fares hopped off to the USA to join his brother, a scrap metal merchant in Providence, Rhode Island. Some months afterwards, mother followed on with my sister and I, travelling steerage on a White Star Liner. She never complained about the hardship of the journey, and in spite of the encumbrance of two babies she managed to make the best of it and find somebody to lend a helping hand.

The new venture was not a success. The scrap metal business could not provide a living for two families so my father went off to work in Montreal. However before too long he was headed back to England working his return passage on a cattle boat. As soon as he had accumulated enough for the fares the family joined him. Settling down must have been a real problem for him because after a brief spell the pattern of the first journey repeated itself, this time to Boston, Massachusetts, again on his own and again the family followed. Twice within their first five years of their marriage they crossed and re-crossed the Atlantic but the turn of the Century saw them back in Liverpool.

My father must have studied English assiduously because he became a fluent public speaker and I remember him as a great reader who devoted much time to the Trade Union Movement. I never knew him intimately, not as my own children grew up knowing me. He never played with us nor did he try to descend to our level. We saw very little of him in the home, he always left for work early in the morning, returning late at night when we were usually in bed and even at weekends he spent his free time with his fellow trade unionists. Sometimes I was sent with a message to his place of work, the dingy, gas-lit, crowded room where men and women slaved away twelve hours a day, six days a week for subsistence wages. There he would sit treading away with his feet, machining together coats for which he was paid sixpence a garment. His trade union involvement was to pay off because, after their first strike, this amount was increased to a shilling.

"My classmates were supercilious at first to this strange creature from a tough school, but I was good at games, could swim like a seal and was pugnacious. This 'Jew Boy' had learnt to put up a fight and could hold his own."

The enlightened age of the forty-hour week, the minimum wage and regular tea breaks were distant dreams of the future. Mass production by new manufacturing methods; ready-made, off-the-peg clothing; the demands of the trade unions and the enforcement of the Factory Acts put most of the

Life After Belsen

sweatshops out of business. Ultimately my father became an enlightened employer himself. He switched from trade union activities to the promotion of working man's insurance against ill health and unemployment. This was a forerunner of the welfare state.

He eventually settled in California after World War I where his brother and step brothers had finally started to prosper. Family history repeated itself and I was left behind in England. Although he had been something of a rebel in the UK, he mellowed on returning to the fold, embracing the conventions that bind Jewish people together and when he died in 1929, his memorial stone bore his name and those of his parents in Hebraic characters and the traditional sign of the divided fingers accorded only to the descendants of the high priests of Israel (Birkat Kohanim).

Growing up in Liverpool, there was a Jewish elementary school but its limited capacity couldn't take the growing population and the overflow had to go elsewhere. I was sent to Pleasant Street Board School and I wonder how many of my classmates would have been considered as delinquents. Coming from dilapidated slum houses that surrounded the school, the boys were a tough lot. The proximity of many Jewish homes to the school provided about a quarter of the pupils, whose parents were mostly immigrants from Russian Poland.

My special buddies, were two sets of brothers, Gentiles

with whom I played truant, roamed the streets and got into many scrapes. Our head teacher, Mr Daniels, ruled us with a swishing cane and a strong right arm. Six of the best, three on each hand, was the normal dose and I was often at the receiving end, usually for insubordination or truancy.

Mr Daniels was certainly an imposing figure. Always immaculately well-groomed in a formal frock coat and pin striped trousers, his appearance in the classroom impelled an instant silence. However, the standard of teaching must have been below average for during my six years attendance only one pupil of the school was awarded a scholarship to a secondary school, a poor record by comparison with other schools and when I left to go to a secondary school at the age of twelve I realised how little I had learnt.

My mother was all for secondary education, having been deprived of it herself, but school fees were a luxury item. Once we were of school age she was not content to stay at home and she pushed my father into several retail businesses, fruit, hardware, drapery, but nothing was successful and my father had to go back to tailoring. Eventually, my mother's two elder brothers, both successful lace merchants, came to the rescue.

As they travelled to Switzerland each year to buy lace, they agreed to supply mother and she rented a stall on market days in Liverpool and several of the Lancashire towns. When market day was on a Saturday, I was roped in, very much

Life After Belsen

against my will, to help at the stall. How I hated sacrificing my Saturdays to serve old ladies with yards of lace while my companions were off playing football!

It was about this time that my father became friendly with a young German, Jewish doctor who had put up his plate in the Jewish district of Liverpool. He was a complete stranger to the UK and gladly accepted the offer to become medical officer to the local branch of the B'nai B'rith, (the oldest Jewish service organisation in the world) of which my father was the president for Liverpool. The members of the society formed the nucleus of the new doctor's practice and it was on his advice and with the reassurance of assistance should it become necessary that I was sent to secondary school to continue my education.

My change of school was a turning point in my life. My classmates were supercilious at first, to this strange creature from a tough school, but I was soon accepted as I was good at games, could swim like a seal, and was pugnacious to a degree. This 'Jew Boy' had learnt to put up his fists to fight and could hold his own!

Chapter 3
The Civil Service
London & Liverpool

Scholastically I had much to learn, I knew no French, Latin or mathematics and had to start from scratch, but within two years I was always in the first half dozen at the end of term. The trouble was that I was lazy and too fond of games. So, I faced a dilemma just before I was sixteen. University scholarships and grants were for the brilliant few, so I had to think of something else.

Two of the boys in my class had taken an open competitive examination in the Civil Service, both were successful and were appointed to Government offices in London as 'boy clerks'. This exam was the Civil Service's

Life After Belsen

ingenious method of providing office staff cheaply for Government departments mostly in London, although there were a few appointments at offices in the provinces. It was open to all British boys between fifteen and sixteen and two thousand young men competed for two hundred vacancies. The successful candidates, on appointment, were given the magnanimous starting salary of fifteen shillings per week, rising by annual increments of one shilling. There were many exceptional young men, some of them did very well both in and out of the service, becoming colonial administrators and even among their ranks a colonial governor or two.

My first appointment was to the Home Office in 1910 where I shared in a humble way, association with my chief, Sir Winston Churchill. It was during his first appointment to cabinet rank, when he became Home Secretary at the early age of thirty-five, the youngest minister in the cabinet. I remember seeing him crossing to Whitehall to take up his seat on the ministerial bench in the House of Commons.

My first impression of the Home Office was somewhat frightening. It was a huge, prison-like building guarded by top-hatted messengers in peculiar red lapelled frock coats, one of which pounced on me and asked me my business. On presenting my letter of appointment I was taken to an anteroom where I waited the arrival of a middle-aged clerk, also in frock coat. Most of the staff, the senior ones especially, wore these coats and top hats. Strangely enough, many years later when I frequently visited the Aliens Branch of the Home Office in Holborn to intercede on behalf of refugees from Egypt after the Suez Affair, the messengers were still wearing the same strange apparel.

The head of department to which I was allocated, the registry, arrived at ten o'clock in the morning, gave me a supercilious glance and took no further notice of me until a clerk appeared with the morning mail. After a short consultation, I was taken to another office and given a small desk on which there was a rather large bundle of newspapers. King Edward VII had just passed away and I was given the menial task of cutting out articles relating to the late king and pasting them into a scrapbook

"My first job was at the Home Office in 1910 where I shared in a humble way, association with Sir Winston Churchill. I recall seeing him crossing to Whitehall to take up his seat in the House of Commons."

Pasting newspaper cuttings was not only an insult to my intelligence, I felt, but the clove-like odour of the paste was inescapable. It followed me everywhere and must have left a scar on my subconscious mind

Life After Belsen

because thirty years later, when the offshore winds from Zanzibar brought the smell of cloves to my nostrils, I imagined I was back in the Home Office, scissors in hand, perusing a mound of newspapers. "The King is dead, long live the King!"

After the funeral of Edward VII, for which I had a grandstand view, from my office window, the obituary notices I had to sift through gave way to items concerning the coronation of George V. Following that I was sent up to the 'rogues gallery' on the top floor, where the records of all criminals, past and present, were carefully numbered, documented and filed, each in its own buff jacket.

My job was to wait near a hand-operated lift, a sort of serving hatch that carried the files to the floors below. The head filing clerk in the main office would receive the requests for certain files, look them up on his register and blow a whistle to attract my attention. He would then call out the numbers of the files he wanted. The numbers often ran into six figures and he could remember a string of them without noting them down.

As the whole of the top floor was used as a registry, and as the shelves were at least twenty feet high, there must have been hundreds of thousands of files. During my many slack periods, for the registry was only aroused from its sleep when a murder was committed, or when a question was raised at the House of Commons about a reprieve, this library of crime was at my disposal, a sort of Agatha Christie paradise!

After several reprimands for dodging off to sit in St James Park, which was situated at the back of our office, I was transferred to the Office of the Special Commissioner of Income Tax, a branch of Somerset House. Lloyd George was then Chancellor of the Exchequer and he had frightened the City by imposing an extra two pence on income tax. The branch office was in Wellington Street at the top of the Strand and I used to take cheques over to Somerset House, then the headquarters of the revenue department.

Life was pleasant in those carefree days of 1910. My next examination seemed so far off. To those of us, away from parental control for the first time, London with all its attractions was too good to be true. Never could so much be seen and enjoyed for so little. Bathing in the Serpentine, jaunts up the Thames, Hampton Court Palace, all the historic places to be explored and when we were flush, the theatres and music halls. Half a crown was ample for a night out. A seat at the London Palladium and most other theatres cost only a shilling. After the show, a meal at a pub would still leave some change out of the original half a crown, with beer at two pence a pint and a bottle of Guinness at the same price, a little indulgence was possible and permissible. The walk home through the West End was an entertainment in itself.

The Bayswater and West Kensington districts were the happy hunting grounds of our kind. Here the landladies catered for our requirements, board and lodging for ten shillings a week. As many as a dozen young men lodged in a house, the catering was simple and often sparse for growing lads, but many of us got parcels from home which helped. The fortunate ones, who worked in the General Post Office (GPO) earned overtime but not us because our working week of thirty-five hours was devised to give us time to study. After a relatively carefree spell in lodgings in West Kensington, my father wrote to me, suggesting I call on his relations, the cap manufacturers to whom he had been apprenticed when he came from Russia. I had never met them and it was with some trepidation that I called one Saturday morning. Being the Jewish Sabbath, the factory was closed.

> *"It may have been a misdirected blow that determined my future career. If my experiences as a boy clerk had been confined to the first three places where I worked, I would have chosen something else."*

They still lived in Spitalfields in the East End, an area mainly occupied by Jews, in the same Victorian house with the factory on the ground floor. As it was Shabbat, my Aunt Dinah suggested that I should stay for the midday meal and meet the family. It was a sumptuous affair by my standards and the furniture in the dining room reflected the wealth of the family business. After we had eaten, my aunt suggested I may like to go and live with her younger sister, Fanny who had two boys about my age. So I moved into Aunt Fanny's house, situated somewhere between Whitechapel and the Tower of London, and her younger son, Harry Newman became my lifelong friend.

It was reassuring to have family in London and I felt a sense of connection but, alas, my halcyon days in the capital were to come to an unexpected end. A severe cold, probably due to a winter dip in the Serpentine could not be shaken and the services doctor ordered me home on sick leave. Following this, I was transferred to the Post Office Engineer's Department in Manchester where I was employed in the registry in charge of records and files. Again, my term didn't last long. The chief clerk was a bumptious, self-important person who tyrannised the clerical staff and spent most of his time prying around the offices.

A colleague and I had come up with a diversion from the nauseating bureaucracy. We would ambush messengers passing through the registry, aiming cardboard cylinders in their direction. One day I struck too soon, it was the boss himself! That was the end. I was suspended from duty to await the decision of the Civil Service commissioner who reprimanded me severely and transferred me to Custom House in Liverpool.

Life After Belsen

It may have been a misdirected blow that determined my future career... after the deadly dull conditions of Manchester the change to the varied and interesting atmosphere of a busy Custom House was quite exciting. It was then the heyday of British shipping and Liverpool was the largest port in the UK in terms of cargoes handled.

Produce from all over the world came through the port. Cotton and tobacco from the USA; meat from South America and Australasia, tea from Ceylon (Sri Lanka) and China, wine from Spain and Portugal and a hundred and one commodities brought in by the White Star, Cunard, Blue Funnel and other famous shipping lines which sailed the seven seas. There were even three and four-masted sailing ships bringing food in from the Baltic ports.

The Custom House, a smoke-begrimed Georgian building with a facade of Grecian pillars and a Wren-like dome was built at the water's edge but the road to the docks now passed between its entrance and the River Mersey. Entering its portals, one was struck by the different smells of wine, spirits and tobacco from the sampling room on the ground floor of the building. The broad, stone staircase led up to the long room, the main office of all Custom Houses, the forum of sea captains and shipping clerks where all documents were lodged and first-hand news from the four quarters of the world, discussed.

Many of the buildings around Custom House had

spacious underground cellars which were used as bonded vaults to store wines and spirits. The iron rings cemented in the walls were relics of the slave trade when our fellow human beings were chained awaiting shipment to the West Indies and the Americas. Cruelly, it was on the back of the slave trade that the fortunes of many well-known Liverpool ship-owning families were founded. Liverpool Custom House did not survive the war. It was destroyed and, with it, the surrounding district.

If my experiences as a boy clerk had been confined to the first three departments in which I worked, I would most certainly have chosen another career, but meeting officers of Customs and Excise, who worked in the outdoor branches, I was keen to join their number and studied harder than ever. In 1914, on my second attempt, I was among the successful candidates of the Open Competitive Examination, the reward for which was a King's Commission as a Customs and Excise officer with a salary of eighty pounds per annum.

Prior to 1910, the two services were separate, each recruiting its own officers and there was an ancient rivalry between them that didn't die with the amalgamation. The excisemen thought themselves a cut above the customs officers, who wore uniforms on duty, and may inadvertently be mistaken for minor railway officials! The excisemen in the country districts weren't overworked, covered their districts on horseback and enjoyed a similar status to that of

Life After Belsen

a country doctor, spending their leisure time hunting, fishing and shooting. In a class-conscious age, to be associated with a uniformed official was not to their liking.

The blow to the exciseman's 'amour propre' (sense of self-worth) came when he was called upon to administer the Old Age Pension legislation. It meant visiting applicants and asking many pertinent and impertinent questions about means and then deciding whether pensions ranging from one to five shillings per week should or should not be granted. In the country, the work was not too exacting apart from its prying nature, but in the towns, most of the work was in the slum areas. Many of the pensioners were bedridden and the appalling squalor of their living quarters called for a stout heart and a strong stomach.

Another hazard was tracking down the pensioner. Any reasonably well-dressed caller was suspicious. He could be a rent collector, bailiff or police officer in plain clothes. In a tenement house, everybody disappeared and went to ground and even in the more respectable districts, the curtains would be pushed aside stealthily before the door was answered. On one occasion, I was presented with a pile of dirty laundry by an old dame who, on realising I had come to investigate her pension claim, was more embarrassed than I was indignant. A spell of pension work gave one no illusions of a utopian England.

Chapter 4
World War I
France & Flanders

The outbreak of the World War I on 28 July 1914 posed a personal problem to all young entrants in the Customs and Excise department. Our contemporaries were joining up to fight and many of us were keen to go with them. However, we were entreated by the Board of Customs and Excise to stay at our posts and promised an early release from our contract. Only those already in the Territorial Army were permitted to go, others who went had to resign. The board stressed the importance of money as a sinew of war and that somebody had to remain behind to do the collection.

My release did not come for a couple of years, but

Life After Belsen

as a salve to our consciences we were permitted to enlist voluntarily prior to the date of our release and, as a further salve, we were issued with a lapel badge proclaiming our indispensability, which was to protect us from female busybodies who distributed white feathers to young men, not in uniform. I was released at the end of 1915 and found myself at Chester Castle ready and willing to 'take the King's shilling.' I had opted to enlist in the Civil Service Rifles but the recruiting sergeant thought otherwise and I was drafted into the Royal Artillery at Fulwood near Preston.

"Religion?" the elderly recruiting sergeant enquired and I recall how perturbed he was when I answered, "Jewish."

"Can't put that down" he said, "We'll just put Hebrew."

To him, the word Jew was obviously only used in a disapproving sense and he had no wish to hurt my feelings.

Incidentally, being a Jew in the army carried some privileges. I escaped the Sunday church parades with their spit and polish uniform code and, as a bonus, received special leave for Jewish holidays. These were, of course, granted subject to the needs of the service.

The Royal Horse Artillery Battery with which I served in France was a fine team of professional soldiers who knew their trade and who were inclined to scorn the amateurs sent to replace their losses, and as I was considered a little too insubordinate to make a good soldier, I had a rough time. I was happiest at the forward observation posts far away from the exacting voice of my sergeant who seemed to like the sound of my name as it rolled off his tongue so often.

To most young men, the foul army language and the crude attitude to the opposite sex came, at first, as a shock, but the uniform and the training soon reduced us all to one common denominator. The appalling conditions of life in the trenches were accepted with a much grumbling however our soldier's irrepressible sense of humour never failed them. The British Tommy's one hope was to get a 'blighty' – a bullet wound sufficiently serious to merit being shipped home to Britain and get away from it all. Even in the great retreat in 1918 when Field Marshal Douglas Haig issued his 'backs to the wall' clarion call there was a sense of relief at the thought that it was all over bar the shouting. When we started chasing the Germans and knew the end was near, the main thought was how much longer it could last.

> *" 'I can't put Jewish down, we'll just put Hebrew.' To him, the word Jew was obviously only used in a contemptuous or disapproving sense and he had no wish to hurt my feelings. "*

In the summer of 1918 when we were attached to an Australian division, we provided artillery support for a much-depleted New South Wales battalion that rooted out a strong

Life After Belsen

German rear guard from Peronne. When the Aussies came out of action a British general addressed them near our gun position showing them on a map how much territory their division had taken since they stopped the rot at Villers-Bretonneux, just outside Amiens. When he finished his eulogy, he asked if there were any questions and a voice from the rear asked: "When are we coming out of the line, you old bastard?" The Aussies were no respecters of persons.

Towards the end of the war, in 1918, my battery had a tough time trying to root out a German rear guard action that was holding up our advance between Peronne and the Hindenburg Line. During this time, I was a signaller, going out each night to patrol the single strand telephone line between the battery and the forward observation post. It was a fiercely challenging job jumping in and out of shell holes trying to find the broken ends of the wire, and I was cynically amused when I received a message from a signaller friend in an adjoining battery wishing me a Happy New Year.

"Just before WWI ended, a treacherous valley filled with mustard gas ended my active service. I was gassed and evacuated to a hospital in Rouen and then to England. My war was over."

Simon Bloomberg

The Jewish New Year (Rosh Hashanah) was about a week off and the thought flashed across my mind that I might ask for leave to attend a synagogue to celebrate the event. I had no idea where the nearest place of worship might be, or whether there was a Jewish chaplain in the field. It was a long shot but it was worth a try. I paraded before my major who passed me on to the brigadier who listened to my story sympathetically and eventually granted me leave. I left the battery, filthy but not forlorn with my rations in a horse's nosebag, glad to get away from the draining pressure of unending war for a few days.

I got a ride with a truck, funnily enough loaded with spearmint chewing gum, and chewed all the way to Amiens. The city was still uninhabited after the German advance in March 1918 and there was no synagogue or chaplain there. So, off I went by train to Rouen where a friendly RASC sergeant arranged for a hot bath, a clean uniform and my first decent meal in months. After the battlefield, it was heaven. Furthermore, I enjoyed attending the French synagogue and when I got back to the battery, ready for action, the sergeant major greeted me with the remark, "Next time I'll join up as a Jew."

A month later towards the end of October, just before the war ended, a treacherous valley filled with mustard gas ended my active service in front of the Hindenburg Line. I was gassed and evacuated to hospital in Rouen and then to

Life After Belsen

England. My war was over.

This was no blighty, a bullet would have been preferable to the burns, blistered skin, sore eyes and vomiting. Known to attack the bronchial tubes, mustard gas strips off the mucous membrane causing bleeding both internally and externally and is extremely painful. I would have problems breathing for the rest of my life, which is why I was always ready to spend time in warmer climates.

It's hard to express the profound effect my three years in the British Army had on my outlook and character. Had I enlisted with my friends and contemporaries, I may have enjoyed the early experiences of training and breaking in, but as I did most of my soldiering with hardened regulars whose ideas were so different to mine, it was no easy passage. Even so I was relieved to be alive, unlike so many of the brave men I fought alongside.

Chapter 5
Chasing the Sun
Kenya & Jamaica

Demobilised from the army on 1 June 1919, the weather was glorious in keeping with my feeling of relief and joy. No more parades, no more restrictions of personal liberty and a month's carefree leave to do the many things I'd dreamt about for so long.

So, off I went on my old bicycle, heading for Southampton and then on to France. The cross-channel steamer was the same one that had taken me across the English Channel three years previously. Landing at Le Havre, I climbed the hill to Harfleur, passing the tented camp that was the much-maligned artillery base camp from which

Life After Belsen

soldiers were sent to the firing line. It was here that the men were paraded, drilled and harassed by a huge sergeant major who fought all his battles and won his medals at base camp.

Heading South to Paris via Rouen, my intention was to travel leisurely, covering about thirty miles a day and stop at French country inns along the way. The favourable rate of exchange, due to the devaluation of the franc, gave me ample funds. Before and during the war the franc and the shilling were almost equal in value. Now the value had fallen to about two pence. However, food and service prices hadn't risen accordingly. A country inn cost little more than twenty francs a night and meals and drinks were correspondingly cheap.

It was a fine summer and the countryside was at its best. My two days spent in Paris were enough sightseeing for me, especially on a bicycle. Many of the roads were still paved with cobblestone which was not the most comfortable form of travel. So I pressed on to Fontainebleau, with its beautiful gardens, before heading home to England.

My return to civilian life didn't present any problems because the Department of Customs and Excise was anxious to get back as many men as it could as soon as possible. I had given serious thought to applying for a Government grant to go to a university to study medicine, but at the age of twenty-four, six years of study and the possibility of not being able to stay the course were too big a challenge so back to the security of a Government job I was glad to go.

Simon Bloomberg

Shortly after the war, I returned to Customs and Exercise in Liverpool. The only drawback was that we had to work Saturdays until one o'clock in the afternoon so the group I worked with made a pact. On alternate Saturday mornings, half the team would work twice as hard and do all the work while the other half played truant and went golfing.

One Saturday morning I was crossing the Mersey from Birkenhead to Liverpool, on my way to the golf course, when I happened to see a boy fall overboard from the ferry into the river. Instinctively, I dived into the filthy water to rescue him, like anyone would have done, especially a former soldier like me, trained to protect and preserve the lives of the people of our nation, at any cost.

I was offered a dry 'Birkenhead Ferries' pullover and a photo was taken of me which was spread all over the Liverpool Echo the next day. The only problem was that my boss saw it, noted the time and I was duly reprimanded! However, a Certificate of Commendation from the Royal Lifesaving Association lightened the blow.

With the right balance of work (including our ingenious alternate Saturdays arrangement) and golf, life was good, but there was something missing and I would find out what that was at a golf club dance. I'd met a young lady named Norah Glover and invited her to a function at the golf club but she wasn't up for dancing that night and sent her sister Alice along in her place.

Life After Belsen

Alice and I soon discovered that we shared the same passion for golf, which gave us an instant rapport. We quickly became great buddies and before long, I proposed to her and we were planning a wedding. However, there was a slight problem. She wasn't Jewish and although that never bothered me, I knew it would be an issue for my family.

Alice refused to marry me unless I told my mother and two sisters first, which I eventually did – just before the wedding. When they heard the news, my mother (Annie Bloomberg who was very much the foreboding matriarch) put endless pressure on me to end the relationship. She of course was trying to pair me off with 'a nice Jewish girl' and when that failed, the rabbi was called in an attempt to dissuade me. A ticket was purchased to send me away to New York but I refused to go.

Finally, the night before the wedding, I was literally thrown out onto the street. I had returned to my sister's house where I had been staying and found my suitcase on the front step along with my other belongings. I can remember the sinking feeling of having nowhere to go, perhaps it would help me in my later dealings with displaced persons as I had a small inkling of what they were going through.

Being made homeless wasn't the end of the world seeing I was leaving anyway, what was far worse was that I had been disowned. That was a hard blow, added to by the fact that I had used my military payout to finance my sister's wedding and now she didn't want anything to do with me. So, it wasn't the best start for Alice and I but we adored each other and I knew nobody else would ever make me that happy. Besides, Alice kept telling me, "You're the nicest person I've ever met, and if I don't have the guts to marry you, then I don't deserve a decent husband."

> *"Despite our different faiths, we decided we would never let religion come between us and were married in a registry office. None of my family came to the wedding."*

Despite us being of different faiths, we agreed that we would never let religion come between us and Alice and I were married at the Birkenhead Registry Office on 12 September 1922, the day after my birthday. None of my Jewish family came to the wedding. It's not how I planned my life to happen but it's often the small and unpredictable events in life that determine one's destiny.

I would later joke with my children that our Bloomberg family may never have happened and all five of them might never have been born had their Aunty Norah not been afflicted with sore feet. So, sore feet determined our future!

It's always sunny on the other side of the street until

Life After Belsen

we get there but the chance of it being sunny is always a lure to those who have the will and the means to go and see. As a young man, I was ever the adventurer and always chasing the sun and, when the opportunity came to take up an assignment in Africa, I jumped at it.

My colleagues and I were standing around chatting at Liverpool Custom House when one of our superiors said that the Colonial Office was looking for a volunteer to go to Africa. Funnily enough, we all applied but I was given the job and Alice was horrified, especially since she had so recently given birth to our first born, Bill on 23 July 1924. Nevertheless, I was appointed senior collector for the Kenya and Uganda Customs Department and we set off to East Africa later that year with baby Bill.

"I can still remember that sinking feeling of having nowhere to go. Perhaps it would help me in my later dealings with displaced persons as I had a small inkling of what they were going through."

Initially we were stationed in Uganda where we settled in the capital, Kampala. We spent two dreadful years there due to frequent bouts of malaria. Despite this, colonial living had its benefits and the African air did wonders for my chest.

Simon Bloomberg

Being in the colonies, one was often 'a big fish in a small pond'. My work gave me a certain level of social standing. The Sultan of Zanzibar was a regular visitor to our house and, when Edward, Prince of Wales toured East Africa in May 1925, I was seconded to be his guide in Mombasa. The island had a close-knit community and our family car was the only one big enough to transport the royal visitor and his entourage. (Little did we know then that when he became king, his reign would last only a year. When I heard about his abdication, my thoughts wandered back to the time I'd met him. Though I was never one for titles, I still felt sad when he gave up on being Edward VIII, became the Duke of Windsor and was exiled to Paris.)

Later in 1925, our first daughter, Marion, who we always called Marie, was born. She and her brother were only a year apart and Alice had her hands full, although the children's 'yaya' (nanny) was a great help. Having been ravaged by mosquitoes in Uganda we returned to England in 1926 in poor health, you could say as thin as rakes. It was during this period of leave that our second daughter, Norah, was born in Birkenhead on 7 May 1926.

After six months of being home in the Wirral, we returned to East Africa. Unfortunately, Bill developed diphtheria just before we left England and had to stay behind with his Aunt Edna. Alice and I headed back to Mombasa with Marie and Norah. Norah was obviously named after her aunt who missed out on courting me! However, she was known as 'Binky' throughout her life, a Swahili term of endearment. Our second son, John Henry was born on 11 July 1927 who we always called Harry and our youngest daughter, Eva May was born in Nairobi on 2 April 1933.

When we lived in Kenya it was divided into two parts, the main colony and a protectorate, the latter being a ten-mile strip of coastal region overseen by the Sultan of Zanzibar, but really under the jurisdiction of the Kenyan Government. The island of Mombasa contains the only port in the coastal strip, Kilindini and is tropical and different in every respect from the highlands of Kenya, in both flora and fauna, and in the tempo at which people work.

The approach to the island provides a delightful surprise that never fails to thrill, particularly at daybreak. First one sees the flashing navigation lights from the shadowy coastline north of Mombasa and when the dawn (alfajiri in Swahili) gives way to the light of day, the dim coastline becomes a long stretch of silvery sand beaches against a backdrop of waving palm trees. The luscious vegetation is simply breathtaking.

The entrance into the Kilindini harbour is through a narrow passage in the coral reef dividing the island from the mainland, past the green fairways of a magnificent golf course built on a coral strip on the island's edge. Kilindini is the finest harbour between Port Said in Egypt and Cape Town in South Africa and it was here that many ships of the British

Navy found shelter in the dark days of World War II.

The colonial lifestyle suited Alice and I and we kept up with our golf. I was secretary of the Mombasa Golf Club for many years and in 1933 became vice-captain of the Nairobi Club. We saw much growth during our time in Africa and I was astounded to see the progress that had been made when I returned for a visit in the late 1950s. I remember how the whole city came out in full force to welcome the first passenger airliner to Kenya when it landed at the Embakasi Airport in Nairobi (now Jomo Kenyatta International).

> *"I was next in line to be the head of Customs and Excise in Kenya but my superior turned out to be anti-Semitic and I was overlooked. Instead I went to Jamaica where I served until 1944."*

When our children started reaching school age we felt we wanted to give them the best possible British education and our four oldest went to boarding school in Keswick in the beautiful Lake District of England. Unfortunately, young Harry became ill and needed several operations done on his ears and Alice and Eva went back to England to take care of him. I returned on leave in 1938 but had to return to work in Kenya shortly before World War II broke out. Regrettably, the war meant that I wouldn't

Life After Belsen

see my family for four years and they would take refuge in Wales without me.

Living in Africa would require great commitment and sacrifice to His Majesty's Colonial Service but Alice and I were prepared to do anything for each other and when we were separated we would always write to each other.

Trying to get back to England in 1942, during the height of the war, I found myself on a leaking ship adrift in the iceberg regions south of Cape Town. Fortuitously my life was preserved and the only damage was that my suitcases were filled with seaweed.

I was hoping to be promoted to head of Customs and Excise in Kenya but my superior at the Colonial Office was known to be anti-Semitic and I was overlooked. However, I did manage to wrangle a posting to Jamaica where I served for the remainder of the war, until 1944 when my time with the Colonial Office was up. As in World War I, somebody had to stay behind to ensure the 'sinew of war' was collected. Besides, close on fifty, I was too old for conscription.

Chapter 6
An Opportunity to do Something Worthwhile

It was a chance conversation on a golf course in Jamaica in 1944 that changed the direction of my life. I was playing with an elderly Englishman, who was an expert in civil administration, sent out by the Colonial Office to advise on municipal reform, which was so badly needed, in Britain's oldest colony.

"What are you going to do when you finish your posting here?" he asked with interest.

My answer was, "I've not yet made up my mind".

"Then why don't you join UNRRA, they badly need administrators," he suggested – referring to the work of the

Life After Belsen

United Nations Relief and Rehabilitation Administration.

That was the beginning of a conversation that was to change my future, my habitat, and more importantly give me an opportunity to do something positive, after what I felt was a life full of negation in government service. Nothingness in the sense that my job as a Customs and Excise official was mainly telling people what they couldn't do. One of my late unlamented chiefs was aptly described as the 'quintessence of the negative' because his natural reaction to a question was to answer 'No'. The negative ploy was always useful when one was not sure how to respond – it gave one time to think!

My time in Jamaica was nearly up, and coincided with the date on which I could retire from His Majesty's Colonial Service should I wish to do so. I held the high-sounding rank of collector general of revenue, and in addition to my main job of tax collector, I spent most of my time as the chairman of a variety of committees whose reports never got beyond the pigeon holes of an overworked secretariat.

One was expected to be an expert on many facets of

> *" 'Displaced Persons', a new species denoting any person uprooted from their homeland and taken for enforced labour or extermination in another country."*

colonial administration, a big fish in a small pond, and being an ex-official member of the local parliament was inclined to give the expatriate officials an exaggerated opinion of their abilities and importance. This may have had something to do with my desire to leave the service at the age of fifty and seek a higher purpose.

I wrote to the director of personnel, UNRRA, Washington, DC, who was the son-in-law of my golfing friend and received an invitation to present myself for an interview in the USA on my way home from Jamaica to England.

Washington, DC in December 1944 was overcrowded with VIPs and it was only with official aid that I was able to book a hotel room, with my accommodation restricted to just five days. The personnel chief was a busy man, but he did find the time to show me around the numerous buildings stretching the length of Pennsylvania Avenue, about a mile long, where in every office typists were hammering away for dear life.

I was suitably impressed but, when the question of my employment with UNRRA came up, there were difficulties. The first UNRRA team was ready to go into Greece to help that devastated Allied country, but a revolution had broken out and they had been marooned in Egypt. Recruitment in Washington had stopped temporarily, so I was told, and I was given a letter to the director of UNRRA in London who would hopefully guide me in the right direction.

Life After Belsen

Somewhat disappointed with the failure of my mission, I decided to visit family and friends in California before returning home to England but air travel was an erratic business in those days unless you were a big shot in the military. Flying often involved waiting or sleeping at the airport in the hope that some general or other VIP would not turn up and there would be a vacant seat.

After a long wait in Washington and a night in Detroit, where I was pulled off the plane at the last minute to give my place to top brass, I eventually arrived in Los Angeles. I didn't intend to stay in LA long but, after a month of trying to get flights, I had to give up on that idea and eventually spent three days and nights on the old Santa Fe train to New York.

This was my second visit to New York. I had first seen the famous skyline on Christmas Day, 1942. After a six month stay in England when the tide of war had not yet turned in our favour, I had sailed from Greenock on 21 December and belted through the Arctic circle, without convoy, and landed in New York four days later.

Now two years later and, after the grim conditions in the UK of the blackout, the bombing and the rationing, New York was a different world. In fact, the differences between the two countries was shocking. The quantities of food and liquor available were unbelievable, even stupefying. Despite the war, not much had changed. The shops were still well stocked and I was able to buy a parcel of food at Macy's to take home to starving Britain.

My return journey on the Queen Mary was with a full complement of American troops, mostly young draftees going over to be at the finish. Rumour had it that there were about twenty thousand on board and from the number of games of Craps going on in every conceivable part of the ship, it certainly seemed like it. There were only five civilians on the entire ship and I was one of them. We were put in the same cabin and I gathered from snatches of conversation that my travelling companions were 'back room boys' who had been working as scientists in the USA. Landing in fog-bound, blacked-out Britain was a little disconcerting, but there was a feeling in the air that the war would soon be over and all our troubles forgotten.

> *"The surviving Displaced Persons (DPs) were the poor unfortunates we were destined to succour and rehabilitate."*

Within a couple of weeks of my return, I went to London to present my letter of introduction to the UNRRA director of supplies at his office in Portland Place. He was most helpful, telling me that I would have little or no trouble obtaining an assignment and passed me on to the recruiting branch. Once again, I had to fill in an application form in quadruplicate, similar to the one in Washington DC, and was told my application would be considered and I would hear back from them in due course.

Nothing happened for more than a month, despite the fact that advertisements for personnel appeared in all the newspapers, and on my next visit to London, I called at Portland Place to see what was happening. I was told there had been a reorganisation of the office and there was no record of my application.

With some persuasion, I filled in another application form and went home. The next morning, I received a telegram asking me to present myself in London for an interview. My interviewers, an elderly gentleman and a middle-aged lady, asked me questions about my work career and experience and decided they would recommend me for a post as director.

About a month later, just after VE Day, I received two communications on the same day, signed by the same person. One telling me that UNRRA regretted that it had no post to which I could be appointed and the other offering me employment as a director, subject to medical fitness. It was evident the office reorganisation had not been a qualified success!

The assembly place for new recruits was 11 Portland Place, where, with several adjoining houses, UNRRA had established its London headquarters, and where for three weeks we were to wander from house to house being processed. Each new batch of recruits was formed into a group. We were Group Eight, numbering about twenty men and women, a polyglot bunch of different nationalities, the men considerably older than the women. It was obvious the war had not left UNRRA with much choice.

Our group was made up of a retired brigadier, slightly shell-shocked; a naval commander of some vintage; a retired Salvation Army adjutant; a Polish former policeman; a Dutch public relations officer seconded by an oil company; an expert caterer from Joseph Lyons; and several others, including one retired fellow who claimed to be a relation of British PM, Anthony Eden, but he did not stay the course.

Our processing started with a series of lectures on the aims of UNRRA, the conception of which we were told, had grown from a speech by Sir Winston Churchill who led Great Britain through the dark days of World War II, when he had promised in 1940 to send food to the enslaved countries.

In 1943, a charter of forty-four allied nations was signed whereby the signatories agreed to subscribe one per cent of their national income towards the running of the United Nations Relief Administration. The extra 'R' for Rehabilitation was added later and thus UNRRA evolved.

A special section of the charter dealt with 'Displaced Persons' (DPs), a new species so named to denote any person uprooted from his or her homeland and taken to work as enforced labour in another country or for ultimate extermination. The surviving displaced persons were the poor

Life After Belsen

unfortunates we were destined to succour and rehabilitate.

For three solid weeks, we received lectures from experts on every conceivable subject under the sun. Professors from London University, the London School of Economics and others gave us the benefit of their knowledge on matters ranging from the calorific values of food to the psychology of conquered peoples. We took notes, studied graphs and statistical tables and were introduced to flow charts that summarised operations and made things seem simple.

The prize flow chart, obviously the conception of some ingenious draughtsman in Washington DC, dealt with every possible type of displaced person and every possible situation and looked like the blueprint of an atomic plant. Very little was said about the actual conditions in Europe or in the camps, or of the extent of the problem. None of our lecturers appeared to have any first-hand knowledge, nor did our headquarters staff seem any the wiser. The final part of our processing was inoculation, vaccination and the provision of a British Service uniform, complete with UNRRA badges and flashes, all ready for our tour of duty in Europe.

Chapter 7
Serving the United Nations
France, Belgium & Holland

On 4 June 1945, UNRRA Group Eight, in full battle dress, led by a beribboned brigadier with a retired naval commander at the rear, set forth for an unknown destination somewhere in France. The following morning, we were at the cliffs of Dieppe waiting to go into the narrow entrance to the harbour, which the Canadians in their daring commando raid had so gallantly breached.

The journey to Paris was enlivened by conversations between an English girl, who before 1938 had never seen England; a French-speaking Mauritian; and a Cambodian doctor, neither of whom had been to France.

Life After Belsen

We arrived in Paris in the evening and, thanks to our uniforms, were able to enjoy an excellent meal at the Cercle Militaire. The next day, we took a train heading north west that stopped at every station to off-load repatriated French POWs being met by their families after long years of separation. Our destination was Granville on the Normandy Coast and on arrival we were taken by truck to the Hotel Normandie, which had been requisitioned as a base headquarters for UNRRA.

From the display of war ribbons, the military was still very much in command and soon everybody seemed to be jockeying for position on the principle of "I'm all right Jack". The soldiers soon made their contacts, the Czechs and Poles sought out their pals and the French, who seemed to be in the majority, were discussing ways of obtaining the much sought-after rations from the US canteen.

It was said that before French president Charles de Gaulle would agree to the Granville Base he had insisted that sixty per cent of the UNRRA personnel at the base should be French. And, from the lively conversations in the long queues already lining up for the much-prized American canteen rations, that seemed a moderate estimate. The oft-used word 'recuperation' indicated that motives in joining UNRRA were not exactly unselfish and in keeping with the noble aims set out by the organisation.

Some months later the French doctor on my team in Salzgitter am Harz left us when he was demobilised from the

French Army. He departed from an adjacent airfield and took the team's medical instruments and equipment with him. This was carrying recuperation a bit too far.

Conditions at the Hotel Nomandie were chaotic with its different languages and numerous staff, the only redeeming feature being the good and plentiful food. We were accommodated in unfurnished rooms using camp beds and our own sleeping bags. My roommate was a Belgian economist from Brussels who knew as little about the workings of UNRRA as I did. He spoke to me in English and I practiced my French on him. We discovered there was a British general in charge of the base, but his suite was surrounded by an administrative barrage through which only a favoured few were conducted.

New groups were constantly arriving, met, as we were, by a white-haired colonel of a Scottish regiment, who gave each party a short speech of welcome followed by a pep talk. On the second morning, I was reading the notices in the hotel lobby when I was invited by the kindly old colonel to accompany him on his daily chores. He suggested that I might take over from him. I consented but one day was more than enough. Speeches of welcome were not my strong point.

The enforced inactivity at Granville, which fortunately only lasted a few days, was a disappointing anti-climax to the hectic three week's of processing in London that had prepared us, so we thought, for service in the field, but there

Life After Belsen

were more surprises and frustrations awaiting us before we could put theory into practice.

Our next move was to Jullouville, a small village on the coast of France, a few miles from Granville, where we found a veritable UNRRA force, probably a thousand strong, milling around in an old school or convent building, the overflow housed in army huts. This presumably was the advance base where teams were formed prior to going into the field.

If conditions at the Hotel Normandie were a bit chaotic, mild anarchy reigned at Jullouville. Sanitation was obviously not part of the training. The squalor in the main building, the blocked drains, and foul toilets, must

"The 21st Army had called for four hundred and fifty UNRRA teams no later than April 1945 to deal with the millions of displaced persons liberated at the end of the war."

have come as a shock to the American contingent. There were many men and women from the USA, seeing Europe for the first time. In the male dormitories, men were lying about on their bunks, unwashed and unshaven, some reading, others arguing, all smoking, the medley of languages adding to the confusion. One look at the place was enough to make the men of Group Eight decide on an army hut, which we could keep

Simon Bloomberg

clean ourselves.

Meal times were a free-for-all, a cross between a rugby scrum and smash and grab raid. We had our meals, good American Army rations on trestle tables, army fashion in a large assembly room. Pieces of bread topped with a square of butter were laid out in each place and we filed past a bench at the door with our plates to get our portions before going to a seat. The first morning I sat next to a woman with a face like a hyena who wolfed down her breakfast, filled her cup and thermos with coffee, drank all the milk on the table, then joined the line to start over. She was obviously on a course of recuperation!

A new series of lectures began for the latest arrivals, this time by speakers that had experience of the assembly centres and camps. A Canadian director who went out with one of UNRRA's first teams and ran camps of Russians and Poles described vividly what we might expect to find. One lecturer, the wife of a one-time British Chancellor of the Exchequer, read us extracts of letters from the assembly centres and camps.

The lecturer of our course at Jullouville was an elderly English don who devised a series of exercises simulating field conditions. He insisted on lecturing in French, to the discomfort of those who did not understand the language. The lectures started at nine in the morning and with two short breaks went on until nine at night and lasted a week. Now we were fully processed, ready to be teamed up and away.

The passing out ceremony over, the directors were instructed to make up their own teams and submit the name and designation of each member to camp headquarters for approval. Each team was expected to have a maximum of eleven members: director, deputy director, doctor, nurse, two welfare officers, supply and messing officers, a secretary and two drivers.

It was not a case of the directors choosing their team but the team choosing their director. All sorts of propositions were put forward, some on the shady side, a warning of collusive acts that were to mar subsequent operations. Eventually after much swapping, arguing and cajoling, the lists were submitted. However, we might have saved ourselves the bother because camp headquarters had different ideas and not one of my suggested names appeared in my team.

Still, Team 299, which I was supposed to lead, was well balanced and had it functioned would have been a good choice of people. Our eleven members consisted of four Dutch persons, two French, three Belgians and two English (myself and a capable Lancashire lass as secretary).

My deputy, Jean, a Belgian businessman, had been an important link during the war in the escape route of Allied airmen on the run. He had kept a photographic record of all escapees who had passed through his hands, evidence enough for execution had he been caught by the Gestapo. Later, when the team was shanghaied in Louvain, we attended a requiem mass for Jean's brother who had been shot by the Nazis.

The doctor, a young Frenchman from Grenoble had a great sense of humour and was a delightful person but he hardly knew a word of English. Fortunately, our Belgian male nurse was a competent interpreter. The two Dutch men were huge fellows, both mechanics and like most Hollanders could speak at least four languages.

Apart from my secretary who did some preliminary work for me, I never had the chance of testing out the merits of my team. We were all good to go but it was another two weeks before the convoy was ready to start its long journey north. There were six teams in the convoy, each with two reconditioned army trucks, one for the personnel and baggage and the other for equipment, stoves, tents, food, medical supplies, gasoline and even drinking water.

We were a self-contained safari. The leader of the expedition was an Englishman who had lived in France since the First World War and he was the only one briefed with the route and destination. My truck brought up the rear and my instructions were to prevent strays and stand by breakdowns. The rearguard was essential because on a previous convoy two trucks, complete with stores and personnel, had headed south towards Paris and disappeared into the blue.

Every two hours we stopped for personal comfort breaks and everybody burst out of the trucks for a leg stretch,

Life After Belsen

scattering into the countryside like hungry sheep in a new pasture. Recuperation started early. Two drivers were caught selling a jerry can of gasoline in a village cafe. After that our stops were made in the open country.

Our route was through the historic battlefields of the Normandy Landing, past Caen where there had been severe fighting and through Villers Bocage, a pile of rubble with only two houses left standing. One had been sliced in two by a bomb and on the remaining bedroom wall an antique grandfather clock hung precariously with its fingers stopped at ten past four as if to register a complaint against the Yankee bomber who put it out of action. The owner of the house, a grizzled old Frenchman, told us without complaint that the bombing on 'D' Day had obliterated the village. As we advanced north towards Rouen, which was to be our first stop, the destruction grew less.

The town major of Rouen to whom we reported, gave us the once over and decided that he had no accommodation for us, directing us to a rest camp twenty miles further on. Once again, we were straggling along, 'en voiture' (by car), like a country circus not quite sure of its next stop.

Military intelligence was incorrect as there was no rest camp but we did come across an ancient castle complete with bastions, towers, portcullis, and moat, guarded by two American GIs to whom we told our troubles. Mesnieres Castle, built in 1042, was being used as an American staging centre for hospital staff. One of the GIs went into the castle and returned after a few minutes with the glad news that camp beds and cooking facilities could be provided for us. Much relieved, for it was getting dark, we humped our kit up three flights of a winding staircase into a large dormitory, where our hosts with usual Yankee hospitality served out coffee and bread and spam.

> *"The hardcore of those who would not return and those who for political reasons could not, the Poles, Balts, Ukrainians, Yugoslavs and stateless and others now remained, and were passed over to the care of UNRRA."*

The second day we passed through the town of Amiens, which had been badly knocked about, and along the Albert Road through places I had known in World War I. The Somme Valley with its fields of ripening corn and its rebuilt red tiled farmhouses was a different place to the waste and destruction I had witnessed. Our next stop was in Lille where we found accommodation in a disused textile factory that had been seconded as a transit camp for passing troops. The following day we crossed into Belgium and reached Brussels early in the afternoon.

Life After Belsen

The UNRRA liaison officer to which we had to report, a grey-haired Irish colonel, was not exactly friendly. He greeted us angrily with the remark, "Who the hell sent you here? I have already issued several instructions to UNRRA headquarters telling them we don't need any more teams."

After much palaver, we were pushed off to an old school in Louvain where, to our amazement, we found all the teams that had left Jullouville weeks ago – at least those who hadn't taken 'French leave' and gone off swanning around the countryside. One look at the place was enough for me. The sooner I got my team on the road again, the better. The military officer in charge of this chaotic mob was a young English captain, who had served in East Africa, so we had something in common. He advised me to continue on to Holland where there was a UNRRA centre near Nijmegen.

We left the following morning, spent a night in Antwerp and landed up the next day at Hattert near Nijmegen, close to the Dutch border with Germany. Here we found more UNRRA personnel, marooned and discontented. The Belgian director in charge of the camp, a very worried person, could give us no information, except that the UNRRA liaison officer to the 21st Army Group was expected shortly, and until he arrived we could do as we pleased so long as we did not stray too far.

My Dutch drivers were natives of Nijmegen and one of them lent me a bicycle, the favourite means of transport in Holland. So, I was able to explore the Dutch countryside and swim in the nearby canal joining the Rivers Maas and Waal. This was an ideal way to spend a sweltering hot July but one had the feeling of cheating, of enjoying simple pleasures under false pretenses.

The liaison officer turned up on Bastille Day, 17 July when many of the French were away in Brussels celebrating their national holiday. He was an Englishman of my own vintage, a veteran of World War I, who had been out in the Far East. He had managed to get away before the Japanese Army arrived and had joined UNRRA in its early days. It was from him that we first learned the truth about UNRRA's operations in the field. At a meeting of the directors, he told us that the 21st Army had called for four hundred and fifty UNRRA teams to come no later than April 1945 and deal with the millions of displaced persons liberated at the end of the war. But, UNRRA was not ready and could only provide one hundred spearhead teams, many members of which were totally unsuitable for the task. The army had therefore formed its own civil affairs branch (DEPACS) to deal with the problem and the bulk of the displaced persons were being repatriated more rapidly than anticipated.

The hard core of those who would not return and those who for political reasons could not, the Jews, Poles, Balts, Ukrainians, Yugoslavs and other stateless individuals, were to now be passed over to the care of UNRRA. The unsuitable UNRRA officers had been sacked from the spearhead

Life After Belsen

teams, which never consisted of more than seven, and now replacements only were required. All teams not already in the field were now to be broken up and suitable personnel sent only as replacements. UNRRA headquarters had already been informed of the situation but still went on recruiting personnel and dispatching teams.

The liaison officer was certainly a man of action. The day following the meeting of directors I was on my way to 21st Army UNRRA headquarters at Wunstorf in Germany, empowered with a letter to the area director appointing me as his deputy. I left like a deserter leaving the members of Team 299 but, as all new teams were being disbanded, the blow wasn't so hard.

One team only was to remain intact, a group of men to be sent to the Island of Sylt where there was a large camp of Polish DPs. I was to travel with them as far as Osnabrück and then hitchhike to Wunstorf. Taking the road north we passed through Arnhem and saw the fateful bridge with its centre span still in the water. We pressed on through the rubble of war, through Zutphen, Lochem, Hengelo, Enschede with its silent factories and crossed the Dutch frontier into Germany at Gronau.

Chapter 8
Aftermath of World War II
Deutschland

We needed no frontier barrier to tell us we were in Germany. The sleek herds of Friesian cattle, all stolen from the Dutch, were evidence enough. Travelling through Holland there was not a cow to be seen. The Nazis, thorough even in their looting, had taken the lot and a small border war was going on between the enraged Dutch farmers who wanted their cattle back and the border guards.

Rheine was the first industrial town of any size we passed through in Germany. It was completely flattened and from there on the towns were utterly destroyed, mountains of bricks and mortar, far greater destruction than I had seen in

Life After Belsen

London and on Merseyside – just complete obliteration.

Osnabrück, where I was to leave the UNRRA team, was our night's stop. We reported to the town major who passed us on to Military Government Civil Affairs, who weren't a bit helpful – all we got out of them was permission to stay in one of the few houses left standing, which was devoid of furniture and all its windows were broken.

A UNRRA director turned up later, an Englishman, who was in charge of a camp of Russians and Poles, ten thousand of them. Both nations were still at war with each other but joined together at night in raiding parties on the surrounding German farms. The director was wearing a holster complete with army revolver, contrary to UNRRA regulations, but, as he said, it helped him to maintain order in his warlike camp.

Every time a batch of Russians was repatriated they celebrated their departure by breaking up the camp furniture, tearing out the wall fittings and throwing everything through the windows. A multitude of German carpenters was constantly employed repairing the damage before the next batch arrived.

That night we heard the rattle of machine guns and the whine of bullets, the miniature war lasting until dawn between the raiders and the British patrols. One irony of the situation was that the British had no jurisdiction over the Russian delinquents who had to be handed over to their own officers.

The following morning, I was fortunate enough to thumb

a lift on a RASC truck going to Wunstorf, my destination. We travelled through intensively cultivated countryside, not a barren patch anywhere, no hedges, no margins of weed. The bumper harvest must have been produced with the labour of displaced persons so ruthlessly exploited by the Germans, because now there were only a few women in the fields, and very few men. The ample supplies of potatoes and vegetables that I had seen in the Osnabrück market made me think of the long queues at home and the 'no potato' notices in the greengrocer shops. Germany would not starve that year.

The area headquarters of UNRRA at Wunstorf was installed in a large well-furnished house providing living quarters for the team and a mess run on regimental lines. The director, an ex-cavalry colonel, spent much of his time visiting the team in his scattered area, smoothing out the difficulties between the army and UNRRA, both approaching a particular problem with different methods.

London and Washington were very anxious to maintain UNRRA as a civilian organisation even to the point of discouraging the wearing of badges of rank among the many soldiers it had recruited under its banner. However, in Germany it could not have functioned without the army which supplied our vital needs, provided for our security and ruled our actions by army directives.

The army maintained, with some truth, that UNRRA gave it many more headaches than the displaced persons. On

Life After Belsen

my arrival, the colonel was 'in conference', so I handed my letter to a UNRRA officer I had met at Portland Place, an ex-regular soldier, who read it and seemed most perturbed by its contents, although he said nothing at the time, except to ask me to wait. The letter was passed on to his chief, who emerged from his office very embarrassed and full of apologies.

He had, he told me, already recommended his deputy for promotion to the post – the man to whom I had handed my letter! After lunch, it was suggested that I should wait at Wunstorf until the matter was referred to London, or if I wanted to, I could take charge of a team in the field.

Three days at Wunstorf watching the acting deputy perform his duties was more

"Most of our time was spent listening to the problems of displaced persons who thronged the assembly centre from early morning till late at night with requests for which there was no answer."

than enough to decide my choice. Drawing Navy, Army and Air Force Institutes (NAAFI) rations, paying the German house staff and acting as the colonel's sidekick was not my idea of relief and rehabilitation. So, as my choice of a field assignment suited all parties concerned, I was transported by jeep to the small village of Salzgitter am Harz about twenty miles south of Brunswick to my first appointment.

My driver, a Canadian welfare officer had temporarily been in charge of the Salzgitter team, whose previous director, a Pole, had been fired for inefficiency and suspected of moral delinquency. The Canadian now promoted to area level introduced me to the team, loaded all his possessions into a jeep and could not get away quickly enough. So, after three months of trials, tribulations and frustrations, I was at last in a position to put into practice all the theory I had absorbed in London and Jullouville.

If my new Team 240 was an example of the spearhead teams, I can understand why the army had such a derisory opinion of UNRRA. The team had no deputy director, its senior member was a grubby French doctor, who hailed from Perpignan and knew no other language than his mother tongue, which he spoke in machine gun like bursts. Furthermore, he spent most of his time careering around the countryside in a requisitioned German car. This was the doctor who, some months later, when demobilised from the French Army, left for his native Perpignan, taking with him the team's medical equipment and surgical instruments.

The supply officer, a veritable 'Flying Dutchman' scoured the surrounding country for loot, getting his inside information from three young German girls lodged in an attic

Life After Belsen

of the UNRRA mess, who were being fed on our rations. The young Hollander seemed to be doing good business because three days after my arrival a German farmer inquired about the validity of a receipt for twelve hundred marks paid by him for a machine purchased from the supply officer. The machine, it transpired, was the village fire engine complete with hose. The following day the supply officer was on his way to the Wunstorf area headquarters with a brief note explaining his redundancy. Nine months later an inquiry came from the military police in Holland asking whether the supply officer, who had been picked up in a stolen jeep, was still a member of Team 240.

Next in order of uselessness was a French warehouse officer, sans warehouse. What he did other than draw the team's NAAFI ration, I never could discover, but he didn't last long. The remaining male member of the team was a Belgian mechanic in charge of the non-existent transport. The few old jalopies requisitioned from the Germans, ready for the scrap heap were invariably out of action, our main means of transport was an army Bedford truck which delivered the daily rations to the camps under our control.

Two Belgian women completed the team, one a welfare officer and the other a nurse of outstanding ability, probably the only member of the team who actually earned her salary. There were also several appendages to the team, displaced persons who helped at the assembly centre, our combined office, living quarters and mess, in the centre of the village. They lived in the camps but were fed in the UNRRA mess and received as payment for their services a weekly portion of the much-prized NAAFI ration. They acted as interpreters, typists, and clerical assistants and helped the welfare officer, the nurse and the doctor.

My prize acquisition, Joe, without whom I could not have functioned, was a young Polish cadet-officer, taken prisoner by the Germans in the early days of the war, in the first blitzkrieg which swept most of the Polish Army into the 'bag' in record time. Joe was just out of school when he joined the army and his adolescence was spent in POW camps, but this did not dampen his eagerness for self-improvement. He was determined to get ahead in life.

Joe had acquired an old English novel written about the slave trade in Africa and taught himself the rudiments of the language. In one camp, which the Poles shared with British prisoners, he tried his self-taught English on a Scottish guardsman and found that he was understood. The Scot provided more modern reading matter and conversation so the ambitious Joe never looked back.

When the war in Europe ended and a call was made for interpreters he volunteered as was able to speak Polish, German and French fluently and was attached to the UNRRA team in Salzgitter. He guided me around the camps, translating my orders and conversations to the displaced persons and

Life After Belsen

obtained information for me, which was essential to the smooth running of the job.

I became very attached to Joe and, when I left Salzgitter nearly a year later, I persuaded him to return to his studies, interrupted by the war, and managed to get him a place at Brunswick University where he studied chemistry. (It was not until 1963 that I saw him again. After graduating he had emigrated to the USA where his energy and initiative had earned him a highly paid post as a research scientist in an atomic energy concern. He was married to a Latvian dentist whom he had met near Salzgitter and they had two children and a home on the outskirts of Los Angeles, where I spent a most satisfying day with them.)

So much for my new team in Germany. The first day in Salzgitter revealed that there was little or no office organisation. No records had been kept and there were no spare supplies. Most of our time was spent listening to the personal problems of displaced persons who thronged the assembly centre from early morning till late at night with requests for which there was no answer.

The day's routine started with a conference at Watenstedt some miles away, where there was a branch of the army's special section to deal with displaced persons and where we were lectured by a young army officer on the filling in of army forms and the interpretation of peculiarly worded army directives. The lectures followed by questions and answers wasted most of the morning after which the directors of the five teams, which covered our district, returned to their respective assembly centres.

There were four UNRRA teams and one British Red Cross team, the latter had been early in the field and its carefully chosen personnel had done excellent work. It was from their leader and his team that we got good advice and sometimes even material assistance. Watenstedt had been the headquarters of the Reichswerke Hermann Göring Steel Combine, a huge concern with mines and factories stretching from Brunswick to the Harz Mountains.

> *"The majority of our wards were Poles, deported from their homeland and forced to work for the German economy. It was the fear of a Russian-dominated Poland that prevented them from going back."*

Each mine and factory had had its own quota of slave labour housed in wooden butted camps, many of them hidden away in the well-wooded countryside. It was said that this huge combine employed over a quarter of a million men and women deported from the conquered territories, most of which had already been repatriated by the army. The hard core, those

Life After Belsen

who, mainly for political reasons were left behind, some fifty thousand of them, still lived in the camps and were now the wards of UNRRA.

Team 240's share numbered about seven thousand in fifteen camps scattered over an area of fifty square miles in the foothills of the Harz mountains, the beautifully wooded countryside bordering the Russian Zone. Most of the camps were centred around Salzgitter but others were hidden away in the woods nearer the mines. The majority of our wards were Poles, miners and labourers, many with their families, deported from their homeland and forced to work for the Nazis. Many of the men had worked in the mines of Belgium and northern France and spoke French. They hated the Russians as much as the Nazis; it was the fear of a Russian-dominated Poland that prevented so many of them going back.

Of the minorities, the Ukrainians and the Balts (Estonians, Lithuanians, and Latvians) were best behaved, their camps were well administered and well-kept and, unlike the Poles, they gave little trouble to the military police. There was no love lost between them and the Poles who regarded them as collaborators, as many had in fact been, but all had one thing in common, they feared and hated the Russians.

There was also an odd variety of nationals who came under UNRRA's banner scattered about the villages, some living in camps, some in houses, Yugoslavs, Romanians, Persians, (Iranians) and even an Englishwoman and her two daughters. She had married a German engineer in South Africa and the family had been caught out by the war while on holiday in Germany. He was drafted into the Wehrmacht and she and the girls had lived in a cottage near Salzgitter throughout the war, hardly daring to open their mouths.

It took me a week or two to find my way around the camps, guided by Joe. His interpreting skills made him indispensable in the Polish camps, giving him added importance, but he never took advantage of the trust I placed in him. He was always discreet and refused to become embroiled in the never-ending political arguments of those who favoured repatriation and those who did not.

Each camp had its own internal administration under the direction of an elected or appointed leader, who along with the camp committee arranged the distribution of rations and any amenities. They were also responsible for the day-to-day running of the camp, the welfare of the people and camp policing. Entertainment was another key responsibility of the camp leader especially during curfews. This included arranging dance nights which always proved popular.

The Nazis were sadistically meticulous in keeping records of their foreign workers even to the extent of tattooing numbers on those they eventually exterminated. Each camp had its own official bureau where detailed records of all its workers were kept on a card index system and those records which survived the burnings and lootings at the time of

Life After Belsen

liberation were used by the camp committees.

Camp 20 was our largest camp, situated in the centre of Salzgitter with a population of about three thousand men, women and children, and a fast-increasing number of babies. It was fly, flea, and bug-ridden, the women spending most of their time swatting flies off the babies, the men lounging around or sleeping in their huts, refusing to help keep the camp clean. As any form of forced labour was forbidden by the UNRRA Charter, other methods of persuasion or incentives had to be tried. "Cleaning the camp," they said, "was the Deutscher's job, not theirs".

> *"The Nazis were sadistically meticulous in keeping records of their foreign workers even to the extent of tattooing numbers on those they eventually exterminated."*

They had slaved away long enough for nothing. The sanitary arrangements in this camp were so bad that the doctor feared an epidemic, which might have spread to the civilian population and the troops, so he insisted upon an inspection by the newly appointed bürgermeister, who, during the visit, was inadvertently locked in a latrine for a quarter of an hour. The following day a German sanitary squad put in an appearance and cleaned up the camp.

Simon Bloomberg

Fortunately, this camp had an excellent secretary, a well-educated middle-aged Polish lady, who spoke French fluently and smoked incessantly. A regular supply of cigarettes therefore, was a major incentive for her to gather all the tedious classified statistics the army demanded on its numerous forms.

There was no lack of furniture, equipment or stationery in the camp offices, much of it taken from the Nazis. There were typewriters in abundance, calculating machines, steel cabinets and stacks of cards and files. It was just as well because UNRRA provided very little. Most of the loot came from the storehouses at the mines, which we ourselves used to visit until the military took over to prevent further looting

The scenes there were indescribable. It was just as if a bulldozer, driven by a drunken driver, had crashed, smashing everything in its path. Papers and records knee deep on the floors, broken machines, and furniture, telephones ripped out of the walls, broken glass everywhere – wanton destruction. Most portable things had been removed and each camp had its quota of loot. All my office stationery was headed Ringleheim, a pleasant nearby village with a Medieval Schloss (castle) and a lake full of pike. The Hermann Göring executives had chosen an excellent location for their offices. Some of the camps made good use of the loot, one, in particular, had installed a shoe-making machine and they had managed to get a stock of leather. Another had a cigarette

Life After Belsen

making machine but the raw material for this was a bit of a problem to obtain.

The general rule was the smaller the camp, the better it was run and the less trouble it gave. There was one exception, which we called 'the hard case camp', into which Joe, my interpreter, would not venture. He maintained that the inmates were criminals released from Polish jails by the Nazis and were afraid to return to their homeland. They certainly lived up to their reputation, raiding German farms, stealing and killing cattle and were constantly at war with the military police.

One of their leaders had discovered a novel way of attracting his prey. Armed with a loaded hypodermic syringe and a concertina, he would creep up to a pigsty at night and make squealing noises. When a curious pig came within range he would give it a jab with the needle and wait until the tranquilliser took effect, then carry off his booty in a sack.

Strangely enough, I never had any trouble with this camp, apart from the occasional military police raids, and I used it as a transit camp for wandering displaced persons, who in their travels between camps, came to the assembly centre for help

July and August passed without any word or visit from the higher echelons. As far as they were concerned we didn't exist. No additional staff, no private mail, no sign of any pay and, what was more important, no sign of the much talked about UNRRA stores for our wards. Although the English press gave accounts of huge UNRRA supplies for displaced persons in Europe, none came our way and it was at the suggestion of the American director of an adjoining team that we travelled on US Labour Day to Frankfurt, the nearest UNRRA headquarters in the American Zone, to see what had happened to our mail and get what further information we could.

> *"In the upheavals that tore people from their homes and scattered them over Europe, each case was its own little tragedy and UNRRA was the benevolent papa to whom each could tell their troubles."*

My companion, Bill Pope from Arizona, believed in the direct approach. He went into the large UNRRA office, banged on the counter and roared, "Where the hell's my mail?" One of the startled clerical staff came to the counter and it transpired that the mysterious address APO 707, to which all our private letters had to be addressed, was indeed Frankfurt, for the clerk produced three bags of mail for Team 240.

While we were sorting it out, a UNRRA official in civilian clothes, a sure sign that he was in the upper strata, asked us many questions about our work and the progress we were making in the British Zone. Bill held forth in true

Life After Belsen

senatorial style, describing the frustration, the lack of supplies, the ineptitude of our headquarters and the stranglehold on our activities by the British military – a favourite theme with Bill.

We were both asked to return after lunch, when we were ushered into a large conference room where the original enquirer was joined by another civilian, who we were informed was on a tour of inspection from Washington, DC. Each of us was asked several questions and our replies were recorded by a secretary.

On the issue of supplies, of which there appeared to be ample in the American Zone, I was instructed to take a letter to the British Zone

"There was a human side to the work the army could never have provided. Such heartbreaking cases could not have been dealt with by military directives."

headquarters directly, ignoring the proper channels. The open letter I carried asked, among other things, why the UNRRA supplies allocated to the British Zone had not been distributed to the camps in our area and demanded early action.

On arrival at zone headquarters, I was told that the chief, Sir Ralph Cilento, a distinguished Australian doctor, was away on tour but one of his deputies would see me. I was kept waiting outside the office a couple of hours and then marched in like a soldier before his commanding officer. The ancient and beribboned warrior who accepted and read my letter scowled and barked at me.

"Have you filled in form number...?"

I replied that I had filled in numerous forms asking for supplies but with the same result. I was summarily dismissed and there ended the matter. Experience had so far proved that London headquarters did not know what was happening at the base in France, or further afield. It is interesting to quote from General Frederick Morgan's book *Peace and War*.

General Morgan played a major part in planning the operations of the 'D' Day landings, and in late 1945 was appointed chief of displaced persons operations in Germany. After a brief and stormy period of office, in which he claimed that he was the victim of American politics he was relieved of his post. His description of UNRRA's London headquarters is as follows:

> My adventures at Portland Place disclosed little that meant anything. I sat in at a number of so called conferences which, for the most part, took the form of impassioned harangues by doubtless well-meaning individuals who each felt keenly and deeply on some matter that was not easy to discern. The authorities at Portland Place could give little information about anything. I could

discover little regarding the extent, the number of displaced persons and refugees to whom I was to administer. Less was known as to the whereabouts of the 'camps' in which they were collected.

While some hundreds of employees had gone might be two hundred, had never been heard of since. The task such as I conceived it to be, was in truth impossible of accomplishment. There was no place for such an outfit as UNRRA to attempt to assume the responsibilities and perform the tasks that could only be the province of the army authorities. What, in effect, UNRRA achieved in Germany was to add considerably to the army's anxieties and offer cover for all kinds of underhanded activities that without the presence of UNRRA those up to no good would have found it extremely difficult, if not, impossible, to pursue their nefarious ends.

Whilst I agree with General Morgan's assessment of the ineptitude of the London headquarters in the British Zone, his wholesale condemnation of UNRRA's activities in the field was not justified. His drastic weeding out of undesirables had a salutary effect, but the invasion of army 'top brass' into the higher posts of UNRRA, which followed his appointment smacked of finding jobs for the boys.

Some were able and took the job seriously, to others it was just an extension of their military duties. The army's attitude towards displaced persons changed considerably after the days of liberation. During the period of non-fraternisation with the Germans, the troops in Salzgitter attended the dances in the camps, and provided transport for the girls, if the dances were held elsewhere. Relations were most friendly, in fact, many marriages between British soldiers and Polish girls were celebrated in Salzgitter.

"In a multitude of disconnected people I tried to reconnect them. Sometimes it was a small gesture, but to them even a small act was huge. At times my contribution was more meaningful, Even so, this was but a drop in the ocean – such was the need."

Later on, when the German girls competed for the favours of the soldiers, their attitude towards the displaced persons changed and, when British troops were called out at night to deal with the cattle raiders or other unruly elements, they began to regard all displaced persons as a nuisance. In Salzgitter, we

Life After Belsen

were fortunate in that the commander of the British troops in our sector was a fine type who went out of his way to help us. The colonel in charge of the Military Government of the Kreis, in which our district fell, was most approachable and used his significant influence on the reluctant Germans to improve living conditions in the camps.

Even the sorely tried security forces were not as harsh as they might have been. There was a human side to the work, so to speak, that the army could never have performed, those heartbreaking cases that could not have been dealt with by military directives.

In the cataclysmic upheavals that tore people from their homes and scattered them over Europe, each case was its own little tragedy and UNRRA was the benevolent papa to whom everyone could tell their troubles, and even if they only got friendly advice, they were assured of friendly protection.

Chapter 9
The Polish & Ukrainian Camps
Salzgitter, Germany

In the autumn of 1945, when Polish repatriation was still in the air, the Military Government wished to ascertain how many displaced persons were living in private residences outside the camps and approached the German civil authorities for the necessary information. In Salzgitter, there was a considerable number of these displaced persons who drew their rations from but lived outside the camps. They were called upon to sign a document declaring that they would either go into camps or accept German citizenship.

When one of the bewildered Poles brought me this strange document, the terms of which I knew to be contrary

Life After Belsen

to the policy of the Military Government, I rang up the town major who told me that he had received a directive about displaced person statistics which he had passed on to one of his sergeants to translate into German, and this strange eviction order was the result. When told that the misinterpretation had put the fear of God into the displaced persons the major replied, "Perhaps I had better cancel it."

The bürgermeister was already preparing the eviction arrangements, delighted at the idea of putting the displaced persons out on the street, with the whole population looking on and the British soldiers standing by to see there was no breach of the peace. Thankfully I put a stop to it.

In the Summer of 1945 repatriation to the East through the Russian Zone had come to a standstill. The Poles were anxious to return, but there were so many reports about Russian influence in Poland that they hesitated, hoping to get first-hand news from the venturesome ones who had gone immediately after liberation, those who had trekked home through Southern Germany and Czechoslovakia to avoid the Russian Army.

The two Polish Governments, one in exile and the other, the Communist-supported 'de facto' government in Warsaw, gave different accounts of what was happening in the country. The daily broadcasts from Warsaw painted a rosy picture of the prospects if only the people would return to help build the new nation, and urged the Polish DPs to form groups of fifty and apply to the nearest UNRRA centre where transport and rations for the journey would be provided.

The irony of the situation was that UNRRA couldn't even provide transport for its own officers. The long battle with worn out army trucks and broken down German cars, for which spare parts were unavailable, lasted as long as I remained in Germany and sometimes reduced us to the indignity of begging lifts from the displaced persons in vehicles they had looted from the Nazis. It was during this interim period, before our first planned repatriation in the autumn that we had so much trouble keeping the peace.

Despite the dusk to dawn curfew, raiding farms, rustling cattle and looting farmhouses went on incessantly. Extra food was in demand for the all-night dances and parties and the frightened German farmers were fair game. Much time was spent interceding with the security forces for our apprehended displaced persons. In one case where a motorcycle was stolen, I stood bail for a young Pole who absconded before the trial. Fortunately for me, the military court was not sure about the judicial arrangements between the army and UNRRA, so no further action was taken.

In another case, a brutal murder in the main street of Salzgitter caused much bad feeling among the villagers. A German civilian taking his girlfriend home from the cinema was set upon by two Poles and murdered. Both men were tried by a military court and sentenced to hanging. It so

Life After Belsen

happened that one of the murderers was an identical twin and so much like his brother, who also lived in the camp, that it was impossible to tell them apart. At the identification parade in the camp, the German girl pointed to the wrong brother, who was arrested and subsequently convicted.

It so happened that the wrongly accused man had been on police duty in the camp at the time of the murder and the camp roster corroborated this. A broken front tooth, the only distinguishing mark between the twins, and the roster established his innocence. An appeal was lodged on the grounds of a miscarriage of justice and following a tense period of waiting, during which the camp expressed its disapproval of all in authority by refusing admittance to all UNRRA personnel, the conviction was overturned. To celebrate the success of the appeal, a party was held in the camp, a Polish bishop from London came to participate in the festivities, and the UNRRA Team were the guests of honour.

"The whole population seemed to be on the hike displaced persons of all nationalities on the move north, south and west – any direction away from the east where relations with our Russian allies were deteriorating."

It was after this disturbing affair that the team arranged its first repatriation of Poles, mostly young men, and women fed up with the inactivity and restrictions of camp life and willing to take a chance. Between seven and eight hundred volunteered to return and to avoid political complications with the Russians, the route was by rail to Bremerhaven and then by Polish ship to Gydnia.

The paperwork involved in this exercise and the strain of the seemingly endless farewell parties left the team exhausted, but the satisfaction of having accomplished part of our task and the happy mood of those packed in the old familiar 'forty men or eight horses' railway box wagons was worth the effort.

The climate seemed right for repatriation on a bigger scale, but for some unexplained reason, UNRRA's directives instructed us to dissuade the Poles from going home for the time being, pending the arrangements for large-scale repatriation under discussion with the Polish Government.

It seemed certain that we should spend our first winter in Salzgitter with our camps still full. Fortunately, reinforcements and replacements for the team began to arrive. Another French doctor to replace the one who had decamped with all our medical equipment; a Canadian supply officer bringing with him two truckloads of essentials, the loot of the early days of liberation, and no less than three deputy directors, all Hollanders, sent for a month's training, at the

Life After Belsen

end of which period I was to retain my choice and return the other two to area headquarters for reposting.

Jan, a tall, good-looking Hollander whose experience in the Dutch East Indies, gift of languages and boundless energy made him an obvious choice was a great acquisition. The team called him the 'Deutsche fresser' (gobbler of Germans) because of his ability to scare the wits out of intransigent German officials who were never cooperative when it came to doing the work ordered by the Military Government for the DP camps.

Jan's experiences in the Dutch Underground left him with little love for the Germans, for whose whining excuses he knew all the answers in the vernacular. He was a great favourite with the displaced persons particularly with the woodcutting gangs organised for felling trees for winter fuel; he could swing an axe with any of them and his popularity was enhanced by his frequent appearances at the camp concerts where he played the violin.

Fortunately for him, he was tall and his large frame could take the special brews of Polish liquors without apparent effect. The Poles seemed to me to be a nation of prolific distillers, able to produce the most devastating 'hooch' from anything that would ferment, and every ceremony be it wedding, funeral, baptism, birthday party or dance, always produced its own special blend of liquid dynamite.

Speeches and toasts were followed by 'nasdrovia'

(good health) or more appropriately 'down the hatch', which demanded a short, sharp movement to the mouth with a full glass, and then a quick gulp. The empty glass was replaced on the table bottom up. To unsuspecting and inexperienced guests this friendly custom was the quickest way to find oneself under the table. My strategy was to choose a place at the trestle table near an open window or recess and sit with my back to it. After the first nasdrovia I raised my glass quickly simulating a gulp but throwing the liquid dynamite over my shoulder. In the dimly lit hut, I nearly always got away with it!

> *"The almighty cigarette had supplanted the worthless mark as the basic currency and was accepted for food, goods, services and favours."*

The welfare section of the team was greatly strengthened by the arrival of Ella, an American social worker of wide experience from Baltimore, who soon organised work in the camps and had her Belgian colleague running around after her like a well-trained poodle. She was petite and paid much attention to her personal appearance setting an example to her team members. She soon had the camp leaders eating out of her hand and being a devout Catholic took charge of the many weddings and baptisms.

Life After Belsen

Another welcome addition to the team was a young British Air Force gunner, just demobilised, who came to us as a warehouse officer, a most important job now that the long-awaited UNRRA supplies had begun to arrive. We now had blankets, second hand clothing and boots and shoes, insufficient for our needs, but it was a start.

The unexpected and heaven-sent gift of Red Cross POW food parcels said to have been arranged by that humane friend of displaced persons, General Eisenhower, one parcel each per month called for a special ceremony at which the first parcel was opened and its contents displayed. Most of the team had not seen such a collection of delicatessen foods since 1939. Each parcel contained sardines in olive oil, tuna fish, canned meats, coffee, sugar, dried milk, chocolate and to crown it all seven packets of American cigarettes. The fags alone were literally worth their weight in gold and were to solve all our employment problems, enabling us to reward our DP workers for special tasks, the woodcutters, the sanitary men, the camp policemen, and the office workers.

The almighty cigarette had supplanted the worthless mark as the basic currency of Germany and was accepted by the Germans for food, goods, services, and favours. The ruling rate of exchange was ten marks for one cigarette, a rate very much in favour of the British Tommies who could exchange the marks in the NAAFI canteens at forty to the pound, thus enabling then to replenish their stocks advantageously.

Simon Bloomberg

It took the British Treasury a long time to discover that German marks were being exchanged for British postal orders and even for war saving certificates at the army post office in Germany, and sent home for encashment. When the Treasury did wake up and issue special army currency for these transactions its losses were substantial.

News of the Red Cross parcels soon got around the camps and the word 'pakiti' soon replaced the mention of recuperation in the daily conversations. The pakiti also helped to solve a problem that troubled the visiting priests and the elders in the camp – inappropriate liaisons between single men and women.

To encourage marriage, we offered an extra pakiti for both bride and bridegroom as a wedding gift to be presented only upon the production of a marriage certificate signed by a priest. The rush of marriages gave the visiting priest a full-time job solemnising the weddings, and one Polish camp broke the record by having a combined quintuple ceremony. Many a pregnant bride was thus assured that her unborn babe would be born in wedlock.

In the frenzied preparations for wholesale repatriation of the Poles, we had little time to think about the future of those of our wards who for political reasons would not go back to their homelands, the Ukrainians, the Lithuanians, Latvians, Estonians, Yugoslavs and other stateless persons left over after the carving up of Europe at the end of the First

Life After Belsen

World War, whose Nansen passports branded them as a new type of nomad whom nobody wanted.

The Ukrainians had a tragic history, divided as they were among themselves. The Western Ukrainians inhabited the province of Eastern Galicia, which before the breakup of the Hapsburg Empire was under Austrian rule. After World War I it became part of Poland, but due to a strong Ukrainian national consciousness, the Western powers secured from Poland the promise that Eastern Galicia would be given home rule within the Polish Republic. This promise was never kept and when the Russians invaded Poland following the Russo-German Agreement, many of the Ukrainians prominent in the Home Rule Movement were banished to deep Russia with no hope of return. Those who were deported as slave labour to Nazi Germany later in the war were classified as Poles, some as Czechoslovaks and others as Romanians and certainly had no desire to return to a Russian-dominated Poland.

"The heaven-sent gift of Red Cross POW food parcels, one per month for every displaced person, called for a special ceremony. Most of the team had not seen such a collection of delicatessen foods since 1939."

Simon Bloomberg

The Ukrainians of Soviet Russia were akin to their Eastern Galician brothers nationally and linguistically, but they were divided by differences of religion and culture – the Polish section were Catholics and belonged to the West, and those in Soviet Russia were Greek Orthodox.

We had camps of both but they kept themselves strictly apart. Our largest Russian Ukrainian camp, Number 49, was on the outskirts of Salzgitter nearest the Russian Zone and had more brains to the square yard than most places in Germany – university professors, doctors, engineers, skilled technicians, nurses, and teachers. I found one elderly professor compiling a Russian-English dictionary on small slips of paper. He had reached the letter 'I', and each completed bundle was neatly preserved in the hope that he might be able to get the book printed later on. When I wrote to Foyles the booksellers in London and got him a second-hand dictionary he literally wept.

This cultural group which came from many parts of Soviet Ukraine was composed of middle-class intelligentsia who had never taken kindly to Communism and when the invading German armies reached the Ukraine, a democratic Ukrainian Republic was declared, willing to help the Germans in their fight against the Communists. The Germans with their usual political stupidity threw all the leaders into jail and deported thousands to work in Germany. The Ukrainians soon learned that they had backed the wrong horse, and now

Life After Belsen

they dared not return to Russia where they would be treated as collaborators, as indeed many of them were.

Under the much-quoted Yalta Agreement of 1945 between Soviet Russia and her Western Allies, all Soviet citizens in Germany, who before 1 September 1939, lived east of the Curzon Line, another tragic demarcation of the Peace Conference after World War I, had to return to Russia, whether they wished to or not. This agreement led to many forced repatriations, too many tragedies and suicides, and it was not until that great American leader, Eleanor Roosevelt had the courage to fight against this decision and have it altered, that forced repatriation ceased.

It was during one of my early visits to Camp 49 that I saw a crowd of agitated displaced persons being harangued by a huge soldier, who from the size of his epaulettes and the hammer and sickle badge was obviously a Russky. Joe stood by me on the edge of the crowd listening to the shouts, the jeers, and the fierce arguments, and because of their mounting temper we pushed forward to ask the haranguer by what right he had entered a camp under the control of UNRRA, an organisation, to which his country made no contribution, nor in fact recognised.

When I addressed him in English he swept me aside with a hand as big as a spade, but when Joe shouted at him in Russian I was grasped in a bearlike hug, patted on the back and greeted with the friendly words "Angelski dobra",

(Englishman good). When asked for his credentials he produced a document written in Russian bearing the signature of General Zhukov, the Russian GOC that he claimed entitled the bearer to enter all DP camps where there were Soviet nationals. I told Joe to tell him in terse soldierly language to get out, and not to come back until his document was countersigned by General Montgomery and to the delight of the crowd he left.

> *"I reacted as I did many times in Germany, whether rightly or wrongly, it is not for me to say, not by rules and regulations, but by ordinary humane instincts."*

It was shortly after this event that we received an army directive instructing us to prepare for repatriation all Soviet DPs in our camps who came under the Yalta Agreement. This bombshell put the Ukrainians into a complete state of panic – some took to the surrounding woods, some threatened suicide, others thronged the assembly centre and refused to leave probably thinking that UNRRA could give them some sort of diplomatic sanctuary.

The directors of the teams in our district who had Ukrainians in their camps decided that would not obey the directive and authorised my colleague, Bill Pope and myself to go to army corps headquarters and say that we would rather

Life After Belsen

resign than carry out the repatriation order. The brigadier we met was sympathetic, but as the directive had come from higher levels there was nothing he could do about it, but he did tell us that in all cases of doubt a military mission would visit each camp and decide who came under the terms of the Yalta Agreement.

This suggested a loophole, highly irregular but we thought justifiable under the circumstances. We called a meeting of all Ukrainians, produced a large map of Europe on which we drew the fateful Curzon Line and then told each person where they lived on 1 September 1939. New DP identity cards were issued to provide corroborative evidence and all was ready for the arrival of the military mission.

When it arrived, it consisted of two officers, one a young British lieutenant who probably had never heard of the Curzon Line, and a dour unsmiling Russian major, both with their interpreters. Each adult displaced person was interrogated and at the end of a long nerve-wracking day not one person in Camp 49 was proved to have lived east of the Curzon Line on 1 September 1939!

Later that year the United Nations acting on a plea by Eleanor Roosevelt decided against forcible repatriation, except for those guilty of war crimes. But the Russians never gave up the hunt for they were determined to catch their victims.

More than a year later when I was the director in charge

Simon Bloomberg

of the UNRRA team at Belsen a Jewish camp policeman brought a message telling me that a 'frau' at the gates of the camp wished to see me most urgently. The heavily-veiled woman was the wife of the camp leader of Camp 49. In an agitated voice, she told me that her husband and the deputy camp leader were on the run from the Russians. There had been another military mission and definite charges of collaboration had been made against the two men. Would I please, please, help them?

They were both hiding in the village and had come to me as their last hope. I knew the personal history of both these men, told to me around their camp table where I had often broken bread with them and knew from their stories that they were decent God-fearing people who hated Communism and all it stood for. Popov the camp leader was a mining engineer born in Kharkov, who had been in trouble with the Russian authorities because of his anti-Communist views, and had been denied the right of residence in seven cities of the Union of Soviet Socialist Republics (USSR).

I knew that he had been prominent in the movement to establish a separate republic when the Nazis invaded the Ukraine where he had suffered imprisonment and then deportation to Germany where he had been employed in the Hermann Göring Works. His wife, a cultured woman and her two young daughters were desperately anxious to learn English in the hope that they might go to Canada where many

Life After Belsen

Ukrainians had settled. The deputy was a mild mannered middle-aged professor who had taught philosophy at Kiev University, who ran the school in the camp. I knew them well, had seen their family snapshots taken in Russia and often discussed with them their plans for the future.

    I reacted as I did many times in Germany, whether rightly or wrongly it is not for me to say, not by the rules and regulations, but by ordinary humane instincts. Fortunately, I knew the leader of a Ukrainian camp near Bremen where for a short time I had an assignment, before going to Belsen, and it was to this camp that I arranged transport for the two men. This enabled them to lie low under different identities until the trouble blew over. Popov and his family eventually found refuge in Brazil.

Chapter 10
Microcosm of the Hunted
Polish Repatriation

There are many stories one could tell about this small microcosm of hunted people, Poles and Ukrainians whose only crime was that they wished to live their own traditional way and worship according to the established beliefs of their church. Two are worth telling because they concern the first two Ukrainians we managed to get out of Germany at the time almost as difficult as a breakout from Dartmoor Prison.

One day in Camp 49 I was chatting with a few elders of the camp, when we were joined by an intelligent-sounding man who answered my Auslander Deutsch in reasonably good English. It transpired that he had been a professor of

Life After Belsen

agronomy at Kiev University, and when I asked him where he had learnt English he told me that his sister had married a British Army officer in Tiflis at the end of World War I and he had lived with them for some time before they went to settle in England.

He had two nieces in the UK, both of which used to write to him up until 1939 but since then he had lost touch with the girls. I wrote to the War Office in England to see if they could help and shortly afterwards the Red Cross search bureau informed me that a niece of the professor had herself been making inquiries about her uncle. She had married and lived in Nairobi, Kenya and offered to sponsor her uncle's immigration into East Africa, an offer supported by the promise of a post as an agronomist to the Tanganyika Government.

Within weeks the numerous formalities were completed and he flew out to East Africa to start a new life. It all seemed so easy that it raised false hopes in the camp, which were to remain in Germany with most of its people for some years. There was a strange coincidence to the story. The name given to me by the Red Cross was 'Fischer', and when she wrote to thank me she said that her name was 'Fisher', and that she was married to an English bank official, a friend of mine in Nairobi, where I had lived for many years.

The second case was stranger than fiction. In the assembly centre office, we employed several displaced persons of various nationalities who had some knowledge of English, principally to act as interpreters for their kinsmen. We had an Estonian stenographer, who was very capable; a Polish cadet-officer; the admirable Joe; a Latvian girl clerk; a Lithuanian driver whose two replies about the transport were either 'kaput' or 'okay'; and a Ukrainian 'office boy' named Pop who was a jovial old gent of at least sixty years of age, always smiling and ready to tackle any job

Pop spoke and wrote perfect English. As a boy, he had been brought up by an English family in Caucasian Russia, when an Anglo-Russian mining company had interests in the Baku oilfields. Trained as an engineer he specialised in coke-oven machinery and he must have been an expert because in the early days of Soviet industrialisation he had been a member of buying missions sent to Belgium to purchase machinery.

It was there that he met an English engineer who had worked in the Caucasus region before the Russian Revolution and who tried to persuade Pop to seek refuge in England. However, for family reasons Pop dared not take the risk. He did, however, give the Englishman certain sums of money, clandestine commissions he had received from Belgian manufacturers, which the engineer placed on deposit in a UK bank. Apart from his benefactor's name and the knowledge that in the 1930s he was connected with an international mining company with its head office in London, Pop could

Life After Belsen

tell me nothing. He was afraid to write to his old English friend because of the strict censorship on all correspondence inside Soviet Russia. With this slim information, on my next leave to the UK, I made some inquiries at the London Chamber of Commerce and finally traced my man to the offices of a mining company in Baker Street. Presenting myself in UNRRA uniform I asked if he remembered Pop. He nearly jumped out of his swivel chair with excitement and wanted to know all about his old friend. I told him all I knew stressing the sordid conditions of camp life in Germany and the hopeless future Pop was facing.

When I asked him about Pop's money, I could see a gleam of suspicion in the engineer's eyes. He probably thought that my motives were pecuniary rather than altruistic. He admitted that a fairly large sum of money was on deposit at the bank and was available to Pop. The problem was how to get it to him. When I suggested that he should

> *"We helped with their problems, kept alive their hopes, gave them the assurance of aid when no help was available, and now had to persuade them to return to their homeland where conditions would not be as rosy as we painted."*

sponsor his old colleague, bring him to England and set him up in a small retailing business, the engineer nearly had a fit.

He said that it would mean hanging around the Home Office for days dealing with the many difficulties officialdom put in the way of would-be immigrants, particularly those from behind the Iron Curtain. My parting shot, perhaps unnecessarily cruel, was to the effect that if he accomplished my suggestion he would at least have one good deed to relate to Saint Peter at the Golden Gate! My intercession must have had the desired effect because Pop was permitted to go to England and later joined his own people abroad.

In the midst of a multitude of disconnected people I tried, where possible, to reconnect them. Sometimes it was a small gesture like giving a dictionary, but to the displaced person, even a small act was huge. Other times I felt my personal contribution could be more meaningful, by assisting them to find a long lost relative who could help in their resettlement, or in Pop's case facilitate the recovery of his rightful property. Even so, I knew this was but a drop in the ocean – such was the need.

The year 1946 brought a spate of new arrivals to the team, replacements, and additions, which seemed strange in view of the much-anticipated repatriation drive expected to decrease the number of our wards by two-thirds. My Dutch deputy, Jan, was promoted to a director post in Hanover. This was a well-deserved promotion, but for me a blow, because in

Life After Belsen

his stead came a gentle Norwegian not tough enough for the exacting work in the camps.

The Canadian supply officer had returned to his home in Toronto, replaced by a blowsy Frenchwoman, a journalist in civilian life, who never stopped talking. We soon discovered that 'recuperation' was her strong point and that she had a working arrangement with the newly formed German Police whom she entertained in her well-furnished room in the mess where she stored her newly acquired gains.

The mystery of her daily disappearances was solved when we had a visit from two British military policemen, who were inquiring about a blonde woman in UNRRA uniform who was scouring the district to blackmail Germans and requisition property. My report of the matter to headquarters brought no reply and I had to connive with the police to threaten her arrest before I was able to dismiss her and off she went with two truckloads of loot.

Two more additions arrived to swell my team to seven. Firstly, an attractive Danish doctor, too attractive in fact, for she married an English major two months later. Secondly a Dutch spinster of mature age and austere looks who locked the door to her room at night, presumably having given up all hope of intruders! She was to be an additional secretary.

The big news was the projected visit to our area headquarters of the chief of UNRRA operations in the British Zone, Sir Ralph Cilento an Australian medico who had the reputation of being a man of action and an able administrator. At the conference of directors, he gave us an outline of future policy and the news that UNRRA would be handing over to another agency at the end of the year, one that would deal with the emigration and resettlement of the hard core displaced persons.

He told us in his decisive Australian manner that he had reduced the number of the teams in the zone from one hundred and sixty to one hundred and thirteen, and after the repatriation drive, which was now being planned, the number would reduce to forty. We were told that over half a million displaced persons remained in the zone, three hundred and fifty thousand of them Poles, the remainder Balts, Ukrainians, Yugoslavs and stateless. The task at hand was to organise repatriation drives in the Polish camps, stressing the advantages of a return to their homeland as opposed to the bleak prospect of remaining idle for years in an unfriendly Germany.

As a special inducement, we were to offer what amounted to several weeks rations, sufficient to cover the period of transport and resettlement in Poland, and extra blankets and clothing were to be added as a bonus. Special missions from Poland were to visit the camps, but with their Russian-like uniforms and autocratic manners these were more of a deterrent than a help.

The sad part of Sir Ralph's story, to my mind, was

Life After Belsen

the news of his impending departure to take up a post with the United Nations. Furthermore, he was to be replaced by an army general. Given all the displaced persons had been through with military control, it was disappointing that the civilian was giving way to the soldier. He introduced his successor General Fanshawe, with whom I would have many differences of opinion. This was the beginning of a military takeover, with brigadiers in all the higher posts, creating a superstructure, military in nature, which regarded displaced persons as units, platoons, and battalions rather than as human beings. It also meant closer cooperation with and subjugation to the Military Government, which was largely uncaring towards the fate of troublesome minorities of displaced persons.

Then, just as we were getting the repatriation drive under way, London and Washington, DC inundated us with an effusion of directives. They wanted to formulate long term plans for rehabilitating displaced persons in the camps providing vocational schools, apprenticeship schemes, the provision of workshops and workrooms, and calling for a census of trades and tradesmen. We were trying to cope with the vast amount of paperwork, nominal rolls and other particulars required by the Polish authorities. It was all very frustrating and a lot of things just didn't make sense.

However, our efforts were rewarded with reasonable success, for on 17 March 1946 Salzgitter Station had its busiest day on record as more than two thousand of our Polish wards were packed into railway wagons, adorned with branches of spring buds, banners, flags, bunting and celebratory slogans chalked on each wagon. Concertinas and guitars played and there was a plentiful supply of home brew to keep the party in high spirits before their departure. For the team, the satisfaction of accomplishment was tinged with sadness. Some of us had lived with them for nine long months, helped them with their problems, kept alive their hopes, given them the assurance of aid when no material help was available, and now we had persuaded them to return to their homeland where we knew that conditions would not be as rosy as we painted. A few Poles who had already been repatriated in the autumn and had returned to the camps spoke of a Poland run by Russian commissars and of a nation destroyed.

> *"This was the beginning of military takeover, brigadiers in all the higher posts, creating a superstructure, that regarded displaced persons as units, platoons, and battalions rather than as human beings."*

Among the repatriates were many whose friendship

Life After Belsen

we cherished, dedicated people whose unselfish efforts had made our task easier, the volunteer teachers, office workers and the woodcutters who had supplied the fuel for the camps the previous winter – we knew them all and would miss them.

The prospect of reorganising the camps and starting all over again was disheartening enough, more so as most of my original team had gone, and the thought of continuing under the hierarchy of 'brass hats' whose numbers had increased as a result of General Morgan's appointment as chief of operations in Germany, was for me, not an inviting one, and I seriously considered tendering my resignation.

It was just at this time that the new area chief, a Scottish brigadier, suggested another assignment to me, to go to a large camp of Poles at Adelheide near Bremen, where the director and his French warehouse officer had been suspended for black market operations. The offer, in view of UNRRA's general policy of retrenchment was in a way an appreciation of my past services and as I had always wanted to see some of the Hanseatic towns from where my maternal grandmother, Bubby had come from, I accepted.

Chapter 11
The Last Jew of Peine
Adelheide & Peine Camps, Germany

The camp at Adelheide was a large barracks, like so many of the military bases scattered across Germany. The camp comprised of two-storey modern buildings; well-equipped cook-houses; shower baths, hot and cold water and flush lavatories. Plus playing fields surrounded the barracks, complete with tennis courts and swimming pools – all the conveniences that made life attractive to Hitler's soldiers.

Now filled with displaced persons, it was clearly evident from the state of the camp that there had been no supervision and it afterwards transpired that the suspended director never left his office to go into the camp and his orders were given to

Life After Belsen

the Polish camp leader through an interpreter.

Despite having some of the best accommodation for displaced persons by far, on my first inspection, the appalling state of the camp made me use language that kept the interpreter in a constant state of apprehension wondering what was coming next. The camp leader was close to tears. The spacious cellars had become a convenient repository for refuse and the flush lavatories were being used for household rubbish instead of the unused garbage bins. Opening and cleaning the drains provided a full-time job for a sanitation squad.

I immediately stopped the distribution of cigarettes until the whole camp was cleared up and each block leader was made responsible for the cleanliness of his building. There was much grumbling at first but when the people saw that I was taking an interest in their living conditions they fell in with the idea of a spring cleaning. To keep the interest alive a weekly competition was started, a special issue of cigarettes was given to the people of the cleanest block.

One thing really shocked me. There was a rather large stock of POW Red Cross parcels in the warehouse that had been ravaged by rodents. The storekeeper had suggested to the previous director that the parcels be opened and the food not in tins stored in rat-proof cases but the director wouldn't agree because he had received no instruction from headquarters. When the parcels were opened, hundreds of rats scurried across the warehouse floor as if whistled for by the Pied Piper. The suspended director was a poor fellow without a mind of his own, who was at the beck and call of the local military major and in consequence was treated like an office boy. He obviously did not know his way around the camp and had probably never been inside any of the buildings. For a couple of weeks, he hung around disconsolately, offering no advice, and I was glad to see the last of him and his partner in crime.

The rest of the team were a mixed crowd, the French deputy, useless, full of excuses for jobs left undone, and most indignant when I told him that under no circumstances would I have him back after his leave, and that I was informing headquarters accordingly. There were two welfare officers one Belgian and one French and a Belgian woman doctor, who had a RAFC major as a boyfriend. This proved useful because he had a vehicle and as usual we had no transport. A recent addition to the team was an American dietician seconded to UNRRA from Heinz (of the sixty-seven varieties). Miriam was a quiet American, a graduate of the University of California, very efficient, full of ideas about catering and eager to put them into practice. Like other executives, she had done most of her travelling by plane and was appalled at the UNRRA transport service. The team lived in the camp immobilised by insufficient transport and suffered from lack of leadership and esprit de corps. No wonder they were all affected by a sort of DP cafard.

The five thousand Poles in Adelheide camp were not anxious to return to Poland despite the visits of many repatriation teams, one of which came directly from Washington, DC a high-powered woman speaker and an ex-GI both of Polish origin. Despite the forceful arguments of this team, the displaced persons were only interested in the stories they had heard about the political state of Poland and the speakers had been warned that they should not to be trapped into discussions on politics.

"The conditions were even worse than some of the Salzgitter camps when I first took over. My whole team was pressed into service and within a week we had the camps reasonably free from vermin."

The non-cooperative attitude to repatriation was no doubt influenced by the presence in a section of the camp of five hundred ex-POW Polish officers, who, would not consider returning to Poland under any circumstances. They had been taken prisoner in the early days of the war and had spent six years doing nothing but walk round saluting each other. Any sort of labour was below their dignity. They lived in the past, hoping for some miracle to restore the old order.

However, judging from the extent of their personal possessions, privately owned cars and bulging suitcases their trips to the black market at Bremen were highly lucrative. They were obviously well paid for their excess rations which were so much in demand. Many of them flouted German girlfriends, the privilege no doubt of officers and gentlemen. When we closed the camp down at the end of April and they left for Gottingen they had at least ten railway wagons to cart away all their stuff.

Just prior to the evacuation of the camp we received news that we were to have an inspection by our new chief, General Morgan who was then touring the British Zone. We got the camp ready for the 'royal inspection', Polish flags very much in evidence, children nicely dressed waiting with bouquets of flowers, but the general didn't come, perhaps his transport let him down!

I never knew what he thought about the organisation until I read his book years later in which he could say nothing good about UNRRA. The general seemed to have a bee in his bonnet about the influence exerted on UNRRA by the American Zionists, whose leaders he compared to the mythical Elders of Zion "plotting to take over the world and overthrow the fast-disappearing British Empire." Like Foreign Minister Ernest Bevin, who, so the general said, persuaded him to take on the UNRRA appointment, he must have had his own peculiar ideas about the solution of the remnant of Jewry still

Life After Belsen

in DP camps in Germany.

The end of April saw the dispersal of Adelheide and the displaced persons who refused to return to Poland went to a 'hard core' assembly centre further north and the POWs south to Gottingen. All UNRRA stores were to be listed, not that there was much to list, and returned and we were to await further orders.

The last scene of all, to end this eventful episode, was the arrival of a cavalcade of horse-drawn transport, farm wagons and covered carts. Surely UNRRA was not reduced to this? Then, as the German drivers came towards us each flourishing a piece of paper, we discovered that the departed Poles had sold and been paid for the official camp furniture, each item carefully listed and now the purchasers had come to collect their bits and pieces. We had to ring up security and net a platoon of Scottish soldiers to clear the camp before we could close the gates and feel secure!

My next assignment was more in the nature of a mopping up operation than a permanent appointment. The team, with certain changes, was to relieve a Salvation Army team based at an assembly centre in Peine, a pleasant little town between Hanover and Brunswick. My supply officer, a French ex-cavalryman and myself were to go in advance, to spy out the land and make the arrangements for the transition.

The Salvation Army team was all female under the guidance of an adjutant, who seemed to work without a plan on an ad hoc basis, doing everything on the spur of the moment. There appeared to be no records kept of any kind, and all correspondence was consigned to the waste paper basket, which seemed the only part of their system that was working!

The assembly centre consisted of six separate camps, the wooden hutted type, some of which had already been cleared and scheduled for demolition, and now they were filled with Poles who had refused repatriation. The conditions were deplorable, even worse than some of the Salzgitter camps when I first took over. In one camp I found an elderly Polish dame sitting on her bed holding up an umbrella to prevent bugs from falling on her head. My whole team was pressed into service and within a week we had the camp reasonably free from both vermin and insect infestation.

My first official visitor was the UNRRA area supervisor, the ex-brigadier, one of the members of my group at Portland Place the year before. We traipsed around all the camps poking our noses into everything pleasant and unpleasant. At one little camp, Peerdorf, which was a shambles, when we took over, the Poles had certainly responded to decent treatment, as most people do.

Two weeks previously they were full of grumbles and grouses, now that their essentials had been supplied, they had transformed the place into a miniature garden city, flowers everywhere, a kindergarten and school going, a handball

Life After Belsen

pitch, and a plot planted with everything from potatoes to tobacco. They considered the visit of a British general a great compliment, the teacher parading her pupils like a proud hen showing off her chicks.

It was at Peine that I came into closer contact with the workings of the Military Government from which I had to obtain stores and equipment to refurnish the camps. The town major, a regular soldier, knew no English and all business had to be conducted through his secretary, a fiery looking Brunhilde, who was the 'de facto' government. She spoke perfect English and when I asked her if she had been to England she replied, "No, but I was specially trained to go over with the German Army".

My muttered reply was unprintable. It may have been sheer coincidence that so many flaxen-haired Delilahs were recruited to serve and provide recreation for Military Government, but it smacked of planned German ingenuity and certainly paid off. The flood of German refugees from the East was assuming embarrassing proportions and all accommodation equipment and food was in great demand and short supply, so displaced persons were relegated to the end of a long queue.

To assist me against the formidable combination of the town major and his secretary I recruited the services of Albert Eichbaum, who had been employed by the Salvation Army team as an interpreter and office worker. He was the only surviving Jew in Peine, where his people had lived for generations, respected citizens, many of whom had attained high civic rank. Albert had been a successful wool merchant, much travelled in Europe and was a man of some considerable means. Like many middle-class German Jews, he was a man of culture, well read and spoke several languages. Perhaps it was because he was so assimilated a German and had married an Aryan wife, who shared his persecution and remained loyal to him, that he had escaped the fate of millions of his fellow Jews. When released from a concentration camp by the advancing Russian Army, he made his way back to Peine hoping to reclaim some of his sequestered property.

> *"Albert had been forced by the Nazis to work in a factory. Now the only surviving Jew in Peine he was being welcomed back by the factory owner as a long lost friend, who said he had been compelled by the Gestapo to mistreat him."*

It was Albert who accompanied me on my begging visits to the Military Government. Albert's story of his first visit to the town hall, now used as Military Government headquarters is worth relating. In the early days of the Nazi

Life After Belsen

regime all Jews had to report at frequent intervals to the bürgermeister or gauleiter and as they entered the portals of the 'rathaus' (town hall) they had to raise their hands in the Hitler salute and say "I ……….. a Jew wish to enter", or words to that effect.

On his first visit to the Salvation Army Camp at Peine, he saw to his amazement some former Nazi employees at their old desks and he instinctively raised his arm to give the Hitler salute. The only difference was that each official had a Military Government (MG) armband instead of the swastika. The chief of police had been the chief Gestapo agent and the bürgermeister high up in the Nazi ranks – now they were all accredited servants of the Military Government.

> *"The major difficulties of our stupendous task in Europe can only be overcome by the continued efforts and self sacrifice that have characterised the work of our field personnel since liberation."*

After the team had reorganised the camps and things were working smoothly the next challenge was to find a house large enough for an office, a warehouse, and a mess. With some difficulty, we obtained permission from Military Government to inspect premises, and with Albert as my guide, I set off to look at a few likely places. Our first visit was to the residence of a manufacturer of brassware to whose factory Albert had been sent by the Nazis to work as a stoker on the boilers. He was forced to toil twelve-hours a day, for which he received a pitiful wage.

The manufacturer to whom we told our business, welcomed Albert as a long-lost friend; he cringed and whined, excusing himself for his poor treatment of Albert, saying that he had been forced by the Gestapo to take such action. Hitler, he said, had ruined all their lives and separated them from their friends, of whom Albert was one. It was all pretty sickening to witness. The house did not suit our requirements and we left the owner in a state of collapse.

Another place we visited was a large country mansion standing in its own grounds, owned and occupied by two steel tycoons and their retinue of servants. The stables and outhouses were crowded with recently arrived German refugees being cared for by the British Red Cross, to whom I suggested that the owners should be moved to the stables and the refugees to the mansion. Part of the house was subsequently appropriated for the refugees.

Just as we got our camps in liveable order with the schools, kindergartens and health clinics all arranged, orders came for a census of all Poles, our main nationality. This meant that each had to state on the census form whether or not they wished to be repatriated, and if not, to give the

Life After Belsen

reason. As most of our wards were illiterate the whole team had to assist in the operation of filling out forms. The result was generally negative and there was only one reason given – the Russkies.

Then came the blow, the last straw, all were to be evacuated to another centre. The reason given for this sudden decision was that displaced persons could only be accommodated where there were security forces and as the army was rapidly being demobilised, conditions were constantly changing. There is a limit to one's frustrations, and the limit had, so far as I was concerned, been reached and I came to the conclusion that there was nothing more I could do at the Peine Camp.

Chapter 12
The Führer's Followers
A Glimpse into their Minds

Just before we left Peine, UNRRA headquarters issued us with an order that completely took our breath away. Everybody had been wondering how they would spend the bank holiday, if we actually got the day off, when much to our surprise we were told we could use UNRRA transport to visit any place we liked for the long weekend, within the district.

Somebody must have had been in a good mood because this was the first time that anything like this had happened at UNRRA and at long last we actually had transport. Our orders were usually of a restrictive kind and possibly had to be because of the attitude of some to 'swan out' all over the

Life After Belsen

countryside at any given opportunity.

With Peine being so closely situated to Harz our team of four decided to head for the mountains. Our transport was a Bedford truck into which we piled enough food to last at least a month or so it seemed and we started off on Friday evening to make for the holiday camp at Altenau that catered for the British personnel in the 30 Corps. We arrived at the rest camp at about nine o'clock hoping against hope to find accommodation, and were met by a charming British officer in civvies who told us that he was trying to pack one hundred and forty-five people into a space that accommodated seventy. So, we continued our journey in the direction of Clausthal-Zellerfeld, one of the highest parts of the Harz Mountains, in the hope that we could find rooms in a German guest house.

> *"None of the German visitors to the guest house had wanted the war. They had been Socialists or Communists or something else, but never Nazis, during the Hitler Regime. At least that was their story."*

Just as we were considering the possibility of sleeping in the truck, we came across a German pub situated at the top of a hill and surrounded by pine forests. It was the residence of the engineer who looked after the turbines on a nearby dam. When we asked for accommodation, a youngish looking man, who apparently was the engineer, said in the German the equivalent of "I'll have to ask my ma."

After some consultation, a rather elderly looking lady offered us the hospitality of a room for the three women to share and a settee in the dining room for me. We were pleased to accept and immediately backed the truck into the yard at the rear of the house and offloaded our kit. We dared not risk leaving our food in the truck overnight, it was too great a temptation.

It was interesting speaking to the German visitors in the guest house, the talk naturally drifted as it invariably did to politics, the Third Reich and the future of Germany. They had been Socialists or Communists or something else, but never Nazis during the Hitler Regime. None of them had wanted the war. At least, that was their story. One wonders what sort of account they would have given, if, God forbid, the war had turned out in their favour.

We had a thimbleful or two of schnapps before we went off to bed and were up bright and early the following morning. After a steaming cup of coffee, we made our way through Clausthal-Zellerfeld down a winding mountain road to Osterode and then on to Northeim. Threading our way through the narrow streets, we were pulled up by a British military policeman who told us we would have to wait until

Life After Belsen

the victory parade had passed.

We had forgotten that it was 6 June and the anniversary of the Normandy Landings and the local troops had staged a march past, probably for the benefit of the Germans. The armoured column, which rumbled past, gave us a thrill of pride. It is always gratifying to see the way British troops turn out so spick and span, and how well everything goes according to plan. It's nice to think that the British can teach others a thing or two about soldiering when we really have to.

Our next stop was Göttingen, a quaint Medieval town more or less untouched by the ravages of war. Here we spent the night with some Polish friends in a military barracks. It was situated on a hill overlooking the town and was surrounded by woods, but completely out of tune with the adjacent countryside. The atmosphere of all barracks is depressing but we were compensated by the hospitality we received from our friends who couldn't do enough for us. They had been expecting us and had gathered wild strawberries in the nearby woods at five o'clock in the morning.

What a tragic problem confronted these poor people who were of officer rank and could not possibly go back to their homeland for political reasons. They had lost everything they possessed, and the future held nothing for them, yet despite this they were cheerful and carried on under conditions that would make most give up in despair.

We got away in good time in the morning and headed

Simon Bloomberg

due south towards Kassel in the American Zone. It was one of those lovely June days, bright sunshine, a fresh breeze and nature showing itself off to best advantage. Even the dull, dreary Autobahn that much boasted about German highway was bedecked with wild roses on either side and the vast undulating land stretched as far as the eye could see. Experiencing this first-hand one could not understand why the Nazis complained of a lack of 'lebensraum'. These vast expanses of wooded lands, when compared with the tiny fields of Holland and Belgium and the miniature patchwork countryside of England made the much-vaunted 'need' for 'living space' seem absurd.

"The rubble of war was much in evidence with black crosses on destroyed buildings as a grim memorial to the many people buried beneath. How easy it is to destroy and how difficult to build up. Man's foolishness knows no bounds."

More so did it seem that day as so many German men were still POWs in Russian hands so there were none to be seen. The few people in the fields were either elderly folk or children. Why the Germans would want to go foraging in other lands when their own was so vast and so beautiful was

Life After Belsen

beyond anyone's comprehension.

A diversion from the Autobahn led us through the town of Hann Münden, a jumble of Medieval houses unchanged for hundreds of years. The rathaus looked like a scene out of a Hans Andersen fairy tale. A UNRRA truck outside the old oak door of the town hall was evidently an event in Hann Münden as we were soon surrounded by a crowd of kids. Then, when the American member of our party committed the indiscretion of giving a sweet to a flaxen-haired mädchen, (girl) the fun began. The children climbed all over us with outstretched hands until we had exhausted our meagre store of sweets in an effort to appease them.

> *"Yes, she'd been a Nazi. 'Why Not? Not everything Hitler had done was bad. Did you not come to the Olympic Games in Munich? And didn't the Prime Minister fly in twice to see the Führer. Why if he was so bad?'"*

Hitler's campaign to encourage more babies was evident everywhere. All over Germany, it was the same. In every town and village there was large numbers of young children. They were once well dressed and well cared for but were now starting to show the effects of undernourishment.

Simon Bloomberg

In the rural districts this was less noticeable, but in the large towns, skinny legs, pallid faces, and dark rings under the eyes told a sad tale of under-feeding. How sad children had to suffer for the sins of their fathers.

The road from Hann Münden to Kassel wound its way through picturesque countryside and villages unscathed by the war and back to the Autobahn as we approached the American Zone. We had no pass into the zone, so we approached the barrier with feelings of temerity, half expecting to be turned back. Imagine our surprise when we came across a German guard in railway uniform standing at the barrier. He took one look at our army truck and waved us on. We had prepared for all eventualities by making the American member of the party don her US coat and cap to convince the guard we were returning rather than coming into the zone. We celebrated the successful passage by singing the 'Star Spangled Banner', but alas, we saw so few Americans that we hardly knew we had changed zones.

The approaches of Kassel had been badly bombed. The British Air Force had certainly left its indelible mark on the buildings of this town. The rubble of war was very much in evidence with black crosses on the destroyed buildings as a grim memorial to the people buried beneath huge piles of bricks and mortar. How easy it is to destroy and how difficult to build up. Man's foolishness knows no bounds.

We drove through the town crossing the River Weser

Life After Belsen

over a reconstructed bridge and decided to head for open country and have a picnic lunch. We halted for a moment at a DP camp flying the red flag and conversed in Auslander Deutsch with some of the Russians who had just come from a church service. They were dreading a return to Soviet Russia, living in the hope of being able to emigrate. The mere mention of Canada set them agog with excitement, their idea of paradise. I did not know what the future held in store for them but I did know that wherever they went they would be an asset to their new homeland.

Branching off the main road, we stopped a farmhand and asked what were the chances of procuring a few fresh eggs. He pointed up a side lane to a large farmhouse saying that the farmer had plenty. Two of us made a frontal attack on the substantial oak door, rang the bell and waited. A uniformed maid, trim and neat, opened the door, listened to our request and went to seek the mistress of the house.

Next came a youngish woman to whom we repeated our request adding that if we could use the kitchen to prepare our lunch we would be most grateful. Again, mother needed to be consulted but we were invited to come in and wait a moment. A distinguished looking dowager of some sixty summers appeared. She spoke perfect English and appeared to be pleased to show off her fluency. She had lived in England forty odd years at Tring Park of all places where her brother had been a zoologist for Lord Rothschild, the first Jewish peer in England. In those far off peaceful days, an Aryan lost no social standing by being employed by 'a now despised son of Israel'. How things had changed in four decades.

We chatted on and she said she could provide us with some fresh eggs and would be happy to let us use her kitchen. So, we called for glasses, poured out a spot of German gin, added a little orange and spoke of many things. She had a houseful of German refugees from East Prussia and had to cater for some fifty people. "Poor souls," she said, "thrown out of their country by ungrateful Poles. Hadn't the Poles come to work on German farms each year, and gone home loaded with good things? What right did these slothful, uncultured people now have to treat Germans so ruthlessly? What base ingratitude!"

"The Führer couldn't have known about all the wickedness that was going on. It was all the work of the SS. The soldiers were all gentlemen and were welcomed by flowers in the conquered territories."

Yes, she had been a Nazi. "Why not? Not everything Hitler had done was bad," she said. "Didn't the British come to the Olympic Games in Munich in 1938 and didn't Neville

Life After Belsen

Chamberlain fly in twice to see the Führer?" she asked. "Why if he was so bad would the British Prime Minister have done that?"

She had seen the Führer once. "What fascinating eyes he had," she said, but added that he had a cruel mouth and she always judged people by their mouths. "Despite this, the Führer couldn't have known about all the wickedness that was going on. It was the work of the SS. The soldiers were gentlemen and were welcomed by flowers in the conquered territories."

When someone ventured to ask what right the Nazis had to conquer the territories, she was stumped for a reply. We let her prattle on. It was probably the gin that was making her talk and it was so seldom that a German person would communicate so freely and unrestrainedly at the time. If only I could have shown her the suffering in just one of the camps I served in. Perhaps if she had the opportunity to meet some of our displaced persons she would change her mind, once confronted with their misery. I would like to think she would have had a different outlook if she could have witnessed the horrors of Bergen-Belsen, which I was about to discover firsthand.

Simon Bloomberg

UNRRA director, Simon Bloomberg.
Simon led United Nations Relief and Rehabilitation Administration teams to assist displaced persons after World War II.

These children survived the Holocaust. Their trousers were made of Nazi flags in protest.
They are cared for here by Simon and a kindergarten teacher at Belsen.

Life After Belsen

Simon and some of his United Nations colleagues in Europe in 1945.
Before going to Belsen, Simon first assisted many Poles, Ukrainians, Estonians, Lithuanians, Latvians in various DP camps.

Simon and team members in UNRRA uniform.

Albert Eichbaum, the last Jew in Peine *(See page 130)*

Simon oversees the repatriation of Polish DPs from Germany.
Music was played and there was an atmosphere of celebration as two thousand people finally embarked on their journey home. (Page 121)

Life After Belsen

Bringing hope to Bergen-Belsen.
Simon was devoted to hearing the concerns of individual Jewish DPs as well as liaising with the camp's Central Jewish Committee.

Simon Bloomberg

From football to drinking tea, from the orchestra to visiting classrooms and chatting to people, he played an active role in the lives of the DPs.

Life After Belsen

Simon as European field director of the Jewish Relief Unit, at Belsen.

Many marriages took place at Belsen after the war and many Belsen babies would grow up to help build the new Jewish homeland.

Simon Bloomberg

The Bloomberg family in England.
*Simon and Alice with their five children
Harry, Bill, Norah, Marie and little Eva.*

In later life Simon returned to the British Colonial Service.
*He worked at the Trade Control Board of Jamaica and
was awarded a CBE in recognition of his years of service.*

Life After Belsen

Simon at Hohne DP Camp in Germany in 1946.
The Jewish DPs refused to call it anything but BELSEN.

Chapter 13
My Own People, the Jews
Bergen-Belsen

On my return to UNRRA area headquarters, I was asked by my area chief, whether I would consider taking on a really tough job.

"It all depends on what it is," I replied. A Scottish brigadier, he was a friendly man with a sound common sense often found among the Scots.

"Would you consider leading the UNRRA team at Bergen-Belsen?" he asked. "We have had three directors in the past few months which have all proved unsuitable for the post. We need someone who can handle a high-level team."

I replied that I would welcome the opportunity and

Life After Belsen

when asked why I said that for twelve months I had worked among displaced persons of many nationalities and this was the first significant opportunity I had been offered to help my own people, the Jews.

I little knew at the time the hazards and the heartaches I was letting myself in for. Instead, my thoughts wandered back to the first Jews I had encountered in Germany, en route from Auschwitz to Belsen. This was such an unlikely mission considering all they had suffered at that notorious camp in Poland to now come to a place in Germany that was just as harrowing. However, they were determined to find their long-lost relatives should any of them have survived. Their plight had troubled me as I had heard of the horrors of the camp at Belsen and now, less than a year later I was being asked to take over a UNRRA team to care for its survivors.

"As if to establish their bona fides they showed me the numbers tattooed on their arms, prefixed by the letter 'A' for Auschwitz, the sadistic method of registration that only Nazi devils could devise."

It was the liberation of the Belsen Concentration Camp by the advancing British troops in April 1945 that revealed the full horror of Hitler's extermination plans and shocked the conscience of the world. My first sight of the camp was in April 1946, when I was taken there by the UNRRA director of Team 806 at Hohne DP Camp who I replaced. All that remained of the hellish place were a few derelict wooden huts, a couple of stone structures which were part of the incinerators, still displaying human bones and many mass graves containing the remains of thousands of victims, mostly Jews.

The survivors had been removed to a military encampment about two miles away, a self-contained small township of modern barracks and buildings hidden away among the pinewoods halfway between the towns of Celle and Lüneburg. The stone-built barracks for the rank and file soldiers and separate bungalows with gardens for the officers, all provided with every convenience, showed how Hitler knew how to look after the welfare of his troops.

The perimeter of the camp was several miles in length and encompassed sports fields, swimming pools, tennis courts, a cinema, two churches and an elaborate building, the Roundhouse used as an officers' mess. It was from here, on a balcony overlooking a spacious ballroom, that one of the most feared men in Nazi Germany, Heinrich Himmler was said to have addressed the Panzer troops for which the camp had originally been built.

There was also a well-equipped hospital to which many of the survivors of the horror camp had been removed when

Life After Belsen

typhus raged and claimed so many lives, immediately after liberation. The hospital was later renamed the 'Glyn Hughes' after the British major and medical practitioner whose untiring efforts saved so many lives.

Although the camp was officially known as 'Hohne' the people refused to call it anything but 'Belsen', and all efforts to dissociate it from the horror camp failed.

The UNRRA director who I replaced had been a member of the Palestine Police Force during the British Mandate and was obviously resented by the Jews in the camp who wished, for the most part, to go to Israel in spite of the British embargo on wholesale immigration. Most of the UNRRA team at Belsen were a dispirited lot. For the few months they had been there they had been frustrated and infected with a melancholia they called 'Belsenitis'. In any case, there was already a spate of relief workers in the camp, three large teams and several subsidiary ones.

The British Red Cross was the first agency on the scene after liberation and as always did exemplary work among the survivors. Then shortly afterwards, a Jewish team from the UK, headed by Lady Henrique went to Celle to work amongst the camp's Jewish population. Later on, the American Joint Distribution Committee arrived with their well-trained social workers and ample funds, followed by Jewish Agency of Palestine who were to train and prepare those who wished to go to the Holy Land. The agency concentrated on the youngsters who were formed into Kibbutzim, communal settlements, where they were taught to be industrious, self-supporting, and instilled with all the moral virtues required by young pioneers going to a Promised Land. There was also an institution called the 'World Ort', which originated in Prussian Poland about the end of the Nineteenth Century to teach Jewish youth trades and crafts, forbidden to them at that time. As all the relief organisations had been coordinated under the UNRRA umbrella, the idea was to send a high-level team to coordinate the work of the various teams and prevent overlaying. This was my new assignment.

> *"This tragic search for the survivors of the gas chambers and incinerators was to continue for years, but for the majority, it was to be a search in vain."*

When I arrived, there were about eleven thousand Jews running their own affairs under the guidance of the Red Cross team. There was also a similar number of Poles, but they left shortly after when it was decided to make the camp an all Jewish one for the British Zone. Previous experience of DP camps did not help much at Belsen. Here everything was totally different. In other camps the UNRRA team did all the administration, welfare, and supervisory work, arranging

Life After Belsen

everything from the distribution of rations and clothing to the setting up of clinics, schools, and recreation centres. All orders regulating the running of the camp were signed by the UNRRA director and were normally obeyed without question. The camp leaders and his committee were elected under the supervision of the UNRRA workers and any of the displaced persons could approach the director if they thought they had been unjustly treated. Here things were different.

At Belsen the real power in the camp was the Central Jewish Committee which was set up shortly after liberation, led by Josef Rosensaft, better known as 'Yossel'. He was one of the unassailable figures thrown up by the chaotic conditions that followed the liberation of the camp. The stories about him were legendary how his spirit and untiring energy saved hundreds of people who had given up on life and would have died. He had the courage of a lion, the cunning of an oriental despot, the vanity of a peacock but the saving grace of a

> *"It was the liberation of Belsen by the British troops in 1945 that revealed the full horror of Hitler's extermination plans and shocked the conscience of the world."*

terrific sense of humour. He spoke Yiddish only and could talk for hours on end, which he did at all times of the day and night. He never seemed to sleep, his small lean body (he was only five feet something) was like a piece of whipcord, and no journey was too much for him and no meeting too long. He ruled his handpicked committee with a rod of iron and though every member was permitted to express their views it was Yossel who had the final say.

His constant adviser and probably the power behind the throne was Dr Hadassah Bimko, a survivor of Belsen, one of the chief witnesses at the military trial that sent Josef Kramer the 'Beast of Belsen' to his death. She used to sit in at all the committee meetings, listening to all the arguments while she was sewing, and from time to time asking pertinent questions. She always dressed in black and reminded me of Queen Victoria in her middle age years. Yossel married Dr Bimko while I was at Belsen and she became Hadassah Rosensaft.

The committee was in permanent session governing all the activities of the Jewish Camp, material, spiritual and recreational, even the medical administration was under its supervision. The committee issued its own ration cards, distributing the basic rations supplied by the Military Government, as well as any additional food and comforts received from the voluntary societies. As food was so important to these ill-nourished people and cigarettes were

Life After Belsen

the basic currency of occupied Germany, the power that was conferred on the distributors of these commodities can well be imagined. To be blacklisted by the committee, as some rival groups were, was a serious matter and few people saw the need to disagree with them.

One could hardly expect democratic action from people who for years had been treated as subhuman and who had to scheme to stay alive. The difficulties of administration were increased by the numerous groups of Jews emanating from different countries of Europe, each forming a minority, and differing in their way of life. The majority were from Poland and they had suffered most. Those from Romania, Ruthenia, Hungary and Eastern Europe had not been deported until 1943 and later. There were Latvian, Lithuanian and Estonian Jews but very few Germans as the German Jews were among the first fatalities.

Differences in physical characteristics disproved the assumption of a single ethnic origin. The Poles were short and squat, the Hungarians, particularly the women were tall and blonde, and the Balts often Nordic in appearance. The Hungarians were a fine crowd, good sportsmen and leaders in cultural activities. Their appointed leader, Rudi, an impresario, was a leading figure in the Belsen Theatre Group. Most of the Hungarians found their way back home to Hungary while I was still at Belsen, but some of the women found refuge in Britain and North America.

Simon Bloomberg

The Ruthenians, an Orthodox group, seemed to have stepped right out of the Middle Ages, their men dressed in long black coats and fur-lined hats with flowing beards. Their spiritual leaders were three brothers, all learned rabbis, who had brought with them ancient scrolls dating back to the Thirteenth Century. The group spent most of its time earnestly studying the Talmud and teaching the younger men.

> *"My first sight of Belsen was in April 1946. All that remained of the hellish place was derelict huts, and the stone structures that were part of the incinerators, still displaying human bones, and the mass graves of thousands."*

One Saturday when I was walking in a remote part of the camp with one of the Jewish doctors of the team, a Czech, we heard strange shouts and songs of exultation coming from one of the barracks. We thought it was a wedding party and went to see what was happening. We were literally dragged in by a bearded rabbi who insisted that we join in the celebration of the outgoing Sabbath and share their meal of rye bread and tinned herrings, eaten with our fingers. All this despite the provision of Kosher food for the Orthodox groups being one of the major headaches of the administration.

One of my first actions on arrival was to call a meeting of the members of the relief organisations; half the camp was still Polish, with a view to co-ordinating the many services and thus prevent overlapping. I knew from past experience that if there were two or more distributing centres for rations and other supplies, it was the easiest thing in the world to get two identification cards and obtain double rations. When I suggested having one single distribution centre, the American Joint, the biggest donor of additional supplies said they couldn't agree because they had a special arrangement with the Central Jewish Committee that they didn't want to disturb.

> *"Although the camp was officially known as 'Hohne' the people refused to call it anything but 'Belsen', and all efforts to dissociate it from the horror camp failed."*

There were many reasons for this arrangement, which I was to discover later. My first contact with Yossel, the camp leader, was typical of many that followed and showed the inner workings of his mind. He came into my office and told me a sad story about the lack of blankets. "Would I ask the

Red Cross for a supply of which they had plenty?"

I fell into the trap with both feet and stormed off to see the stores officer of the British Red Cross, who calmly told me that the Central Jewish Committee tried this periodically, and they had already received ample supplies provided by the American Joint.

Our first real brush came when UNRRA sent a small supply of cigarettes and chocolates for distribution. I had my doubts about the correctness of the numbers in the camp, although I used to sign the ration requisitions without question, so I asked the welfare officers to get the particulars from the leaders of each block of buildings. Little did I know at the time that I was treading on dangerous ground and that my action immediately made me suspect by the committee. Within half an hour of the issue of my order, Yossel was in my office with his secretary, Laufer to tell me that all stores for distribution were his concern and had to be handed over to the committee.

My reply was that the supplies were from UNRRA and as their official representative it was my duty to see that every displaced person in the camp got their fair share. The scene that followed was one I was to witness many times during my stay in Belsen. Yossel stormed and raged, said that he didn't want UNRRA at the camp and I should take myself and my lousy rations and leave!

Once calm returned, he agreed he would supply me

Life After Belsen

with a record of the number of people in the camp and told me it was pointless to try and get this figure from any other source. My reply was that if he wouldn't cooperate I would send the loudspeaker van around the camp announcing that UNRRA had sent cigarettes and chocolates for distribution but the committee refused to allow them to be distributed. Not a very promising start. I was soon to learn why Yossel wished to conceal the numbers in the camp.

About a week later I was called over to the part of the camp recently vacated by the Poles. There I observed a scene reminiscent of the early days of UNRRA when we were confronted with thousands of foreign slaves unkempt, unwashed, half-starved and clad in all kinds of makeshift clothing, from discarded uniforms to Hessian bags.

The new arrivals were Jews of all ages, including children, and they all appeared to be in a desperate state of exhaustion, their clothes tattered and mud-stained. I moved among them asking where they had come from and how long they had been on their way, but the sight of my British service uniform must have prompted them to respond with a determined "Zog em nicht", (Don't tell him anything).

These were the advance guard of many thousands of devastated Jewish Refugees who were to pass through Belsen in the following months. After the Molotov-Ribbentrop Pact, when Poland was divided between Germany and Russia, the Jews in the Russian portion were sent to the East to work in

Simon Bloomberg

the mines and lumber camps. Those who survived were, in 1946 given the option of becoming Soviet citizens or being repatriated to Poland. Most of them chose the latter and returned to find a desolate Poland with no signs of their relatives and with little to keep them there. They were not welcomed by the Poles and there was an outbreak of anti-Semitism that culminated in a pogrom at Kielce. The tragic result was that thousands of Jews streamed across the Polish border to Czechoslovakia, then into Austria and the US Zone in Germany, while many others arrived at the British Zone via Berlin. These were the people that General Morgan spoke of when he said that there was a pre-arranged plan to embarrass the British Government by bringing thousands of Jews from Soviet-occupied Europe for transportation to Palestine. He described them as being well dressed and having plenty of money, but those who came to Belsen were not in this class, and their valuables were non-

> *"The stories about Yossell were legendary, how he saved hundreds who had given up on life. He had the courage of a lion, the cunning of an oriental despot, the vanity of a peacock but the saving grace of a terrific sense of humour."*

Life After Belsen

existent. The committee and the Jewish relief workers spared no efforts to ensure all newcomers were settled in and fed, and I for my part handed over amenities for distribution amongst them.

However, the situation was complicated by a directive from the Military Government that instructed all UNRRA directors not to admit any new refugees into the camps nor provide them with rations, but to send them to the local German authorities for food and shelter. Apart from the fact the German civilian ration was considerably lower than that of the displaced persons, the idea of asking Jews to go to their former exterminators for succour was asking too much. The directive aroused indignation among the people at Belsen, who agreed to share their rations with the newcomers. This was of course why the Central Jewish Committee was reluctant to provide specific numbers.

> *"The idea of asking Jews to go to their former exterminators for succour was asking too much. I decided to adhere to UNRRA's policy which did not differentiate between refugees and displaced persons, and to register them."*

Simon Bloomberg

I had to file a report on the influx of new refugees to UNRRA zone headquarters and send a copy of my letter to the appropriate army headquarters, informing them that it was my intention to carry out UNRRA's policy, which did not differentiate between refugees and displaced persons, a policy carried out in the US Zone.

The negative attitude of the Military Government in the British Zone to this new influx could be understood because the feeding of the civilian population was a severe strain on its limited resources and we had no large reserves like the Americans. However, I felt we could not turn them away and the UNRRA administrative buildings were soon besieged by crowds of refugees clamouring for the registration cards that would entitle them to the special scale of DP rations, and more importantly, enable them to live among their own people in the camp.

My reports to UNRRA and army headquarters were unanswered, except that I received a cryptic signal from the army instructing me to remove the refugees from the camp and punish six of them with the maximum penalty, whatever that was, for illegal movement. As I had neither the means nor the desire to carry out this instruction I decided to adhere to UNRRA's policy and register the new arrivals, and at the same time send an SOS to the UNRRA director in Berlin to prevent him from sending more refugees.

It was just as well that I did because the grapevine got

Life After Belsen

working and each night for the next week we had a new group of arrivals. Several thousand were added to my ration lists and I sat back to await the consequences. This action in defiance of instructions changed the attitude of the Central Jewish Committee to the UNRRA team to the extent that we were no longer treated as persona non grata. The camp magazine printed and produced by the committee finally accepted our presence in an article entitled 'Unser Sztime' (Our Voice).

> "There has been much disagreement between the Central Committee and UNRRA, which is an institution to help people. Our representatives have had to fight to arrange anything. The fault has lain with the UNRRA directors, men without sentiment for our past and they have shown hostility to the Jews. We have noticed a difference since the new director, himself a Jew, has come to Belsen."

Chapter 14
Life at Belsen
Surviving the DP Camp

The dramatic increase in refugees came at a time when I was just beginning to find my way around the Belsen Camp. The barrack blocks were so much alike, that for a newcomer it was a complete maze, and so extensive an area that an internal bus service operated to take the volunteer workers to their daily tasks. When I first took over there was a thriving open-air market in one of the barrack squares, complete with stalls. It was a miniature Petticoat Lane, where an astonishing variety of commodities was displayed, unobtainable at that time in most countries in Europe!

Some of the articles came from the US canteens, the

Life After Belsen

post exchanges, as they were called, but most of the goods came from the store of hidden loot still in German hands, pillaged from the overrun countries of Europe. Cigarettes and coffee, the basic currencies, were in plentiful supply at Belsen, so the Jewish aptitude for trade in a restricted field produced surprising results. This open black market gave the many VIP visitors a false impression of camp conditions so the committee instructed the camp police to break up the market and the stallholders retired with their illicit wares to open shops inside the barracks.

The shoemakers, the tailors, the dressmakers, the leatherworkers and other craftsmen did a roaring business. Where the raw materials came from nobody inquired. It was not only in the camp that the Jews exercised their new-found freedom. Fresh fish for the traditional Sabbath meal always seemed to be in good supply, and although one man was found with a three-foot deep carp pond in the large cellar underneath his room in the barracks, this limited supply could not account for the camp's substantial Friday night consumption.

The mystery of the modern miracle of multiplication of the fishes was solved by accident. The Jewish Relief Unit had on our team a remarkable cockney gent, Izzy, from the East End of London, a jack of all trades who supervised maintenance, sanitation, and the hundred and one jobs so essential in a camp of this size.

Simon Bloomberg

It was Izzy who discovered the carp pond while investigating the cause of dampness in the cellars. And, it was one Thursday, when looking for the refuse collection truck that daily emptied the camp's bins, that he ran into it in a secluded part of the camp. Three workers were sluicing the truck down and cleaning the inside. The reason, it transpired was that every Thursday night the truck was driven to Hamburg ninety miles away, arriving at the fish wharf at dawn in time to purchase, with cigarettes, a truckload of the night's catch, and take it back in time for distribution and preparation for the Sabbath meal.

This was innovative enough, but the supply of kosher meat for the Orthodox community presented even greater difficulties. When the Jews and Poles shared the camp, the Poles did the cattle rustling, raiding the German farms, and sold the live beasts to the Jews for ritual slaughter. Dodging the military police was a hazard that necessitated many stratagems, particularly the final entry into the camp. One method was discovered, again by accident, when one of my deputies saw an ambulance enter the camp through a seldom-used gate.

He asked the German driver where he was going and was told that a kranke frau (sick woman), was being taken to the camp clinic for medical treatment. The deputy, not convinced, opened the rear door of the ambulance and was rewarded for his curiosity by a flick across the face from a

Life After Belsen

cow's tail. The kranke frau had four legs!

Later the Military Government arranged for a quota of beasts to be dispatched, in accordance with the Mosaic laws by the accredited 'shochets', those rabbinical gentlemen especially trained for the job. Permits were issued which had to be endorsed by the UNRRA director, and I can recall one bearded patriarch who came to renew a permit, which had been cancelled because he had already rejected two slaughtered cows on some obscure ritual grounds. While I was writing out a fresh permit, he faced towards Jerusalem and prayed loudly and fervently, obviously to convince me of his piety. Later I discovered that the rejected beasts had been sold to a German butcher at a considerable profit!

"In an place like this, one had to forget normal standards of behaviour. People who had kept themselves alive by strange and tortuous ways could hardly become model citizens overnight."

Another incident that proved I was no match for some of the Talmud-trained operators happened one day when a venerable patriarch came into my office and quite seriously asked me for a permit to enable him to travel to New York to attend an important religious convocation. Travel for displaced persons was severely restricted and going to the USA was about as difficult then as going to the moon, unless one was a VIP. Feeling somewhat facetious I wrote out a permit on official UNRRA paper, using the usual jargon: "To whom it may concern" and requesting that all facilities should be granted to the bearer on his journey to New York. I signed and sealed it with the UNRRA stamp and handed it over. I was unconvinced but it was gratefully received.

At the mess that night I related the incident and we joked about whether it would make any difference. A month or so later I received a call from the quartermaster of military stores at Celle, who asked for my name and then demanded to know, in no uncertain terms, what right I had to sign an army requisition order authorising the issue of several dozen pairs of vests and underpants. I denied the vigorous impeachment, but when the requisition was sent to me for my inspection I discovered that the bearded patriarch had cleverly used the travel permit and grafted my signature and the UNRRA stamp onto the military form. He had then arranged for someone in service uniform to present the document and obtain the clothing. Furthermore, he had somehow made several copies of the permit and sold them to others!

This lesson in cunning and ingenuity was one of the many I learned in the early days of my apprenticeship. It was the older Jewish men who were engaged in these business

Life After Belsen

transactions. The younger men were nearly all members of a Kibbutz, in training for the journey to the Promised Land. They were taken in hand by the teachers of the Jewish Agency who imposed rigid discipline on all who passed through their classes. These youngsters did their own chores, their own cooking and lived as they would be expected to live in 'Eretz Yisrael'.

Soldiers of the Jewish Regiment serving with the British Army, who were stationed at Bielefeld were frequent visitors to the camp and did excellent work training these fine youngsters. When volunteers were required for woodcutting to supply the hospital and other welfare institutions it was to the Kibbutzim that I often turned. The idea of working without reward did not appeal to the older entrepreneurs. I once found a displaced person who had borrowed the camp saws and axes and then engaged several Germans to cut timber for him, paying them with his rations and cigarettes. The wood was then sold to other displaced individuals. He was quite indignant when the wood was confiscated and sent to the hospital to be used as fuel. In an environment like this one had to forget normal standards of behaviour. People who had kept themselves alive by strange and tortuous ways could hardly be expected to become model citizens overnight.

The crowded days never seemed long enough, not to mention the crowded nights, when the committee always seemed to have its lengthy meetings to which the leaders of the relief organisations were invited and expected to attend. The long arguments conducted in Yiddish lasted for hours but a clear-cut decision was rarely made, there was always some reservation. Time meant nothing to those who had lost all sense of time. The most unwelcome distractions and perhaps the most trying, were the visits of numerous parties of VIPs that came on conducted tours around the British Zone. The old Belsen horror camp was always on the itinerary, and as we were nearby, they usually landed up with us. There were British MPs, US Senators, a horde of journalists looking for news stories, and various do-gooders who all came in their droves – all full of suggestions and bright ideas.

> *"Labour's win in 1945, had raised hopes a more liberal attitude might be adopted towards Jewish refugees who wished to enter Palestine, but it continued with the policy of restriction that exacerbated Jews worldwide."*

The rank of the official guides depended upon the importance of the tourists and they were usually conducted around our camp and shown all the welfare clinics, the schools, the workshops and the recreation centres, and were given a quick glimpse of life in

Life After Belsen

the barracks.

One party, a bevy of bishops and important clerics of various denominations arrived followed by a fleet of cars with enough personal baggage to cover the main deck of an ocean liner. The guide had lost his way and brought them to us instead of the horror camp. They refused the usual tour of our institutions because, the guide said, they were pushed for time. When I suggested that his holy wards were more interested in the dead than the living, they were of course annoyed. They did, however, condescend to visit a couple of our establishments, including an orphanage where we had about fifty Jewish children who during the troubled years had been hidden and cared for by Polish families.

A Catholic priest showed pleasant surprise when one of the youngsters bowed his knee, crossed himself and kissed the hem of his holy garb. The priest commented that the Holy Father throughout history always had a soft spot for the Jews, which brought forth my uncalled-for remark that my memory went as far back as the Spanish Inquisition.

One of our distinguished VIP visitors was Victor Gollanz, author, and publisher, who was on a five-week tour of Germany in connection with the Save Germany Now movement. He little realised at the time how soon Germany would save itself, once it got rid of the incubus of the Control Commission which had taken over from the Military Government.

Simon Bloomberg

It was amusing to see the galaxy of 'brass' that turned up to welcome him, a colonel, a couple of majors, a civilian from the Control Commission and my own area chief. They were to act as his guides, but when I told Gollanz that if the people saw the 'Pips', they would not speak, Gollanz firmly told the guides that they were no longer required. They were most displeased when they saw us walking off together on our tour of inspection. We had a pot luck lunch with some of my DP friends, a glass or two of home brewed schnapps, and chatted with all and sundry.

One thing I remember about the visit was the liberal use he made of a large white handkerchief to keep out the unaccustomed odours as we passed through the living quarters. Strange how one becomes hardened to such trivial things. I had long since lost my sense of smell.

Some months later we had a visit from a United Nations Commission reporting on displaced persons in Europe, headed by a Canadian. The party arrived several hours after schedule, surrounded by an impenetrable barrier of red tabs, and did not get beyond the administration offices where they interrogated Yossel, the camp leader and a few displaced persons, after which they were bustled away for lunch in Hanover. We never saw or heard anything of their report; the only memory that remains of that distinguished party is the ten gallon Stetson hat of one diminutive delegate from a Central American Republic who as he departed expressed the

Life After Belsen

opinion that "the people in the camp were very well off".

Our most unwelcome visitors, they seemed to be ever present, were the MI5 snoopers forever trying to discover the sources and members of 'Aliyah Bet', the secret organisation that planned and arranged illegal emigration operations from Europe into British Mandated Palestine.

The Labour Party's shock win in 1945, had raised great hopes that a more liberal attitude might be adopted towards the hundreds of thousands of displaced Jews that wished to enter Palestine, but the new Foreign Minister Ernest Bevin thought otherwise and continued with the policy of restriction that exacerbated Jews all over the world. Time has proved that as a political expedient Bevin's policy was a failure, and from a humanitarian point of view, we in the camps considered it indefensible.

"The only place that accepted the refugees without any reservation was Israel. She would take the sick, the lame and the blind, every Jew who wished to come and let them live as human beings among their own people."

It was common knowledge Belsen supplied its quota

of those who tried to run the blockade in the Mediterranean, operated by the ships of His Majesty's Navy, which resulted in filling refugee camps in Cyprus, itself in the throes of a struggle for independence. News sometimes leaked through that one of our volunteer workers had finished up in a camp in Cyprus, but the matter was never openly discussed. I never made any inquiries, since it was no business of mine, and there was never any attempt by the inner circle to take me into their confidence. My sympathies were naturally with those who tried to get out of Germany. How could they be otherwise?

Most of the people in Belsen had been incarcerated in camps for years, some in Germany others in Poland and Russia, the younger ones could hardly remember any other existence. The allocation by His Majesty's Government of four hundred exit permits per month to Palestine for Jews in the British Zone was sadistically given the name of 'Operation Grand National', probably because it was the most difficult course in British horse racing, and it made no difference to our constantly increasing numbers.

What hopes had these Jews for the future, where else could they go? Britain had taken a generous quota of refugees from the Nazi regime before the war, and in 1946 a considerable number of displaced persons for work in the mines and heavy industry, but there were few among the surviving Jewish people at Belsen who were able to do this

Life After Belsen

kind of work.

In any case, the vast majority wanted to shake the dust of Europe from their feet. Many would willingly have gone to North or South America, but the offers and acceptances were few and far between. To mention a typical case, the Canadians sent a delegation to inquire into the possibility of recruiting tailors. Two candidates from Belsen applied, one a Polish Jew who had spent years in Russian labour camps, and the other a German Jew who had miraculously survived many concentration camps. The former was rejected because he may have been indoctrinated by the Communists and the latter because he might have had Nazi sympathies before he was incarcerated. The Canadian immigration officer had the last word and there was no appeal.

The only country in the world that offered refuge without reservation was Israel. She would take the sick, the lame and the blind, every Jew who wished to come, give them food and shelter, and the opportunity to live as human beings among their own people. Those in Belsen could never understand why Britain, which had magnanimously made possible a home for Jews in Palestine by the Balfour Declaration in 1917 should now prevent them from going there.

Chapter 15
Let My People Go
Eretz Yisrael

In 1946 the outlook was exceedingly grim, more Jews were flocking into Germany, there were clashes between the British Troops and Zionist settlers in mandated Palestine and Foreign Minister Ernest Bevin was determined to carry on with the restrictive immigration policy. All these factors had a disheartening effect on the people in the camp, who openly expressed their anti-British views. However, never at any time was any hostility shown to the British Tommy. The Belsenites never forgot how much they owed their liberators, who were always welcomed into the camp and the Scottish major in charge of camp security was respected by all.

Life After Belsen

Early in September 1946, a Court of Inquiry descended on the camp, brigadiers, colonels, interpreters and staff from UNRRA headquarters, to investigate our increase in numbers, notified by me three months previously and to probe, if possible, the vexing question of 'illegal emigration'. I accepted full responsibility for the increase in numbers, claiming that I was carrying out the policy of UNRRA, my employers, and I told the Court of Inquiry that if that policy couldn't be continued I had no option but to tender my resignation by way of protest.

The inquiry which assumed the appearance of a court martial lasted all day. Yossel, the camp leader was called in for interrogation but with his usual adroitness refused to admit that there was any difference in status between the new arrivals and the others, saying that they were all Jews and all had the one desire, to go to Palestine. The problem he said, could be solved overnight, and the solution was in the hands of the interrogators to 'Let My people go.'

The outcome of the inquiry was a decision to have a census of the camp population, to which Yossel and his committee agreed, subject to certain conditions. The committee was to arrange the tallying points and there was to be no interference with the movement of people in the camp on the day of the census.

On the appointed day a host of interpreters, mostly men from the Pioneer Corps, took up their stations and began the count. Each person was questioned, his or her DP card inspected, and the details recorded. The operation continued until far into the night, the counting tables lit by candles supplied by the committee. When the last of the queues was finally accounted for, the totals approximated the figures shown on the daily ration lists, and honour was restored. The enumerators however may not have been aware that the committee had posted its own tellers outside each of the counting huts, where they had instructed a number of people to register twice and even three times in different places, giving them spare DP cards with different names. Nor did they know bus services had been laid on from Hanover and other places where there were smaller Jewish camps. Still, everyone seemed satisfied and the ration list numbers were accepted as correct. The only casualty, a sad one for the camp, was the removal of the popular Scottish major.

> *"The desire of the vast majority in the camps was to go to Eretz Yisrael, the land of their fathers, where they knew they would be accepted without quota and without restriction, if Britain would let them in."*

It was just after this incident that the director general

Life After Belsen

of UNRRA, Fiorella La Guardia paid a visit to Germany, but Belsen the largest camp in the British Zone was not on his itinerary. The nearest he got to us was Hanover, where there was a camp for a few hundred Jews. Perhaps the atmosphere was too explosive and he had no wish to be embroiled in arguments about emigration.

All the special precautions taken to safeguard the chief from unauthorised intruders did not prevent Yossel from breaking through the cordon and popping up before La Guardia with whom he conversed in Yiddish. A former New York mayor, La Guardia had also been an immigration officer on Ellis Island and could speak the language fluently. On Wednesday, 30 October 1948 an article appeared in *The Daily Telegraph* and *Morning Post*, extracts from which are noted below:

Mr La Guardia Appeals to the USA to Lead Britain on Palestine. (New York, Tuesday)

Mr La Guardia, director general of UNRRA stated here yesterday that if the United States set the lead by allowing one hundred and fifty thousand Jewish refugees to enter the country, Britain would be forced to modify her Palestine policy.

I have ruled that the Jewish people infiltrating into the western zones of Germany and Austria are entitled to UNRRA care as displaced persons. The British military authorities in Germany deny them DP status and refuse them shelter and food, I personally took up this matter with Prime Minister Clement Attlee, and sought to prevail upon him to accept our interpretation of the agreement in international conferences, but the British Government refused to change its policy. Therefore, these people are crowding into the American Zone.

QUOTA ALLOCATION PLAN

I have submitted a plan that would permit the allocation of unused immigration quotas for a short period, to provide a haven for them. I am confidently hopeful that if the United States would take one hundred and fifty thousand to one hundred and seventy-five thousand the United Kingdom would then change its present restrictive policy on immigrants into Palestine.

Britain will do nothing until the United States does something. Brazil has presented a plan, Canada and Australia will surely follow our example as soon as we have our share of these unfortunate people.

Life After Belsen

La Guardia's hopes were not realised. The United States was vociferous about Britain's refusal to allow increased immigration into Palestine but did little to open her own gates. The other possible sources were more interested in selective schemes that chose only the fortunate few and rejected the many.

Politics bedevilled the issue, the Jews in Palestine knew that an increase in their numbers would add to their strength in the inevitable struggle against the Arabs, for Israel's Independence and it was said American Jewry supported immigration on a large scale, provided it was into Palestine and not the USA. However, the deciding factor was undoubtedly the desire of the vast majority in the camps to go to Eretz Yisrael, the land of their forefathers, where they knew they would be accepted by their own people without quota and without restriction, provided Britain would let them in.

> *"I accepted full responsibility for the increase in numbers, claiming I was carrying out official UNRRA policy and if that couldn't be continued, I had no option but to resign."*

The end of 1946 brought no relief, not even a tiny streak to the dark horizon. The food situation in Germany became worse necessitating a reduction in rations to all displaced persons unless they had suffered Nazi persecution.

Our first intimation of this decree was the visit of a Control Commission officer who informed us that from a certain date our rations would be reduced. The usual battle of words ensued, and after the usual lengthy meeting with the committee, a petition was sent to the regional commissioner who ruled that all Jews in the camp should be treated as persecutees and receive the special rations.

Meanwhile, an UNRRA official arrived from the headquarters in the US Zone, to survey the situation and offer suggestions about the future. He was a Los Angeles journalist, whose job it was to coordinate Jewish affairs in the camps in the American Zone where there were nearly a quarter of a million Jews. His immediate reaction was "What's your problem? In our zone, we have ten times the number you have here?" The suggestion was that the whole population should be removed to the US Zone, however this was firmly resisted by the central committee. They would agree to one removal only and that was direct to Palestine.

Politically, they said, Belsen was too big a nuisance to the British authorities to be given up so easily. So, the struggle went on, with the people as political pawns. In the troubled months that I was at Belsen I made many changes but I felt we never really achieved UNRRA's original objective of being overall coordinator because the camp administration

Life After Belsen

was almost wholly in the hands of the committee. The two UNRRA doctors, both Jews, ran their clinics in the camp and worked with the medical staff at the Glyn Hughes Hospital. Our welfare workers fitted in their activities with those of the Jewish Relief team, who were connected with the committee.

My job resolved itself into one of liaison between the committee and the Military or Control Commission. Belsen was the 'hot potato' that nobody seemed to want to handle. Despite many pressing invitations our chief in the Zone never once put his foot inside Belsen while I was there.

It was almost impossible to juggle what I knew to be right, fighting for the rights of Jewish refugees from Eastern Europe when I was being told to turn them away. Ultimately, I was forced to resign in protest and even when the zone chief received my resignation and wished to offer me alternative employment, our meeting was arranged at Celle the nearest township. I of course declined but did agree to stay on at Belsen until a successor was found.

For many reasons, I was sorry to go. Although I had no illusions about my importance in the Belsen scheme of things, which would go on as before when I had gone, I wanted to continue at the camp because I had so many friends among the people, who used to come and discuss their problems, hopes and dreams with me.

There was the mother whose two sons had left on one of those illegal drafts and finished up in a camp in Cyprus.

Simon Bloomberg

Could I get them back?

There was the case of a young Jewish ex-soldier who had fought for five years with General Anders and taken his discharge in Palestine where he had worked as a weaver in a textile factory, until the troubles put him out of a job, and he had applied for repatriation to Poland to join his wife and family. He eventually found them in Belsen and asked to be allowed to join them. When he was informed that this was not possible and that he would have to register for food and shelter with the German authorities he flung his British Army paybook and identification disc on the table and shouted: "Are you meshuga? (crazy) Or am I?" What could I answer? I had to let him stay.

> *"Belsen DP camp was so different from the other camps in which I had served. The many activities, mental, physical, recreational and spiritual all bore witness to the urge of the people to fit themselves for the future."*

Then there was the dear old lady who had been hidden for a year in a Polish convent who came to Belsen because she thought she might be able to join her two sons in Palestine one of whom was a distinguished surgeon. In these cases,

Life After Belsen

there was only one solution, the illegal issue of a DP card and fortunately my registrar Bim, a Polish Gentile was of the same opinion as myself.

There was something about Belsen that was so different from the other camps in which I had served. There was none of the apathy, none of the hopelessness, none of the feeling that they were living on charity, that corrupter of morale; for all they received was only a small part of what was taken from them. The many activities, mental, physical, recreational and spiritual all bore witness to the urge of the people to fit themselves for the future.

There were several schools at Belsen DP Camp, both primary and secondary, a technical school, a teaching seminar, a people's university and several religious training establishments. Also, there were no less than six different sports clubs, several football and boxing teams and gymnastic classes. There was a dental mechanic training centre under an enthusiastic American

"I was sorry to go for many reasons. Although I had no illusions about my importance at Belsen, which would go on as before, I wanted to carry on as I had so many friends who used to come and discuss their problems, hopes and dreams."

teacher, and there were training courses for nurses.

The theatrical group put on some excellent shows one of the best being Sholem Aleichem's 'Bewitched Tailor', the amusing story of the befuddled husband and the billy goat. Permission was obtained for the company to take a tour of Belgium and France where they were enthusiastically received. Even politics was not neglected in the camp. There were at least seven political parties corresponding to those in Palestine and during camp elections posters and slogans were plastered all over the place.

One could not help admiring the virility of people that had survived the Holocaust that had just destroyed six million of their kinsmen in Europe.

My successor arrived in time to allow me to get home to England in time for the year-end holidays, but before I went I was approached by the American Joint Distribution Committee, whose British Zone headquarters were in Belsen, with an offer to direct the US affairs in the zone. I accepted immediately, subject to being permitted a spell of leave in England. Eighteen months living with displaced people was a sort of Kafka experience that had warped my judgement to the extent that I felt I had become somewhat more displaced than my wards.

Any qualms I had about serving under the Stars and Stripes were quickly put to rest by the refusal of Control Commission to allow me to return as a camp leader employed

Life After Belsen

by the Americans. When I wrote to the chief of DP Division at Control Commission, who had always been helpful to me, his letter, quoted below, was unequivocal and decisive.

> "Dear Mr Bloomberg, your case has been fully discussed. I know of the good work you have put in at Hohne but I am sure that you will realise that with so many people in the zone with one society and another endeavouring to circumvent the policy we have to enforce, an official who has once resigned from work with displaced persons because of an expressed unwillingness to cooperate with the policy of the occupying authorities, cannot be surprised if the occupying authorities are not willing to accept him under another guise to carry on the same work."
> – General Kenchington

So that was that. I had to agree with the 'justice' of the decision. So ended my time with UNRRA, but not my connections with Belsen or my commitment to serving my people.

Chapter 16

Back to Belsen

The Jewish Committee for Relief Abroad

A period of rest with my youthful family did much to restore me to normality. Life in Britain although austere was, away from the towns, restful and pleasant, and gradually the mental scars of the past two years began to efface themselves.

Occasionally I got a jolt when the odd letter brought news from Germany. I had promised to give evidence, if necessary, on behalf of a captain in the Jewish Brigade stationed at Bielefeld, who during a visit to Belsen, was apprehended and put under arrest by the military police for filming in the camp. A wire from the War Office informed me that neither my evidence nor my presence was required.

Life After Belsen

What happened to the officer I never discovered.

Then quite out of the blue came a letter from the Jewish Committee of Relief Abroad, the governing body of the British Jewish Relief Units in Europe (voluntary workers sent out from Britain) asking me whether I would consider taking the job of field director in charge of their units in Germany and Austria.

The JCRA was the executive relief organisation financed by the Central British Fund and like other British relief organisations subsidised by the Foreign Office. I had not yet reached the stage of thinking about future employment, so the invitation to return to relief work had a strong appeal. I accepted the offer, subject of course, to the lifting of Control Commission's ban on my return to Germany.

On 12 May, 1947 I was on my way back to Germany to take up my new post. As the JCRA came under the UNRRA umbrella I had to report to the European headquarters in Paris to obtain my clearance to enable me to enter Germany.

The UNRRA headquarters staff shared the Hotel Majestic with the staff of UNESCO, in a calm detached atmosphere so different from the hectic fields of operation. The future of UNRRA was still undecided and many of its able officers were resigning, leaving the old 'shellbacks' and 'barnacles' that would stay on until they were prized away.

The officials were very helpful and in a couple of days, I was on the train going through the ghost towns of the Ruhr that Bomber Harris had reduced to mountains of rubble. The railway stations in Germany at which we stopped were crowded with people better dressed than those in England, and almost everybody without exception carried a briefcase or a suitcase, so necessary when foraging on the black market.

> *"One could not help admiring the virility of people that had survived the Holocaust that had just destroyed six million of their kinsmen."*

The countryside was at its best, the tidy hedgeless fields like a patchwork quilt, and the orchards in full blossom, so great a contrast to the blasted towns. Two years previously I had entered Germany by the same route, but by road, and then the whole countryside was one huge market garden, every possible scrap of land under cultivation. Now the foreign slaves had gone, much of the land was lying fallow, and only women and old men were in the fields. So many of the men were still in the East, unable to return.

I disembarked from the train at Osnabrück where a German porter assisted me with my kit and gushed when I gave him three cigarettes as a tip. A phone call to the Unit headquarters at Eilshausen, my future abode, brought a Ford service van within a couple of hours, driven by a cheery

Life After Belsen

British ex-sergeant enrolled by the unit.

Eilshausen was one of those pleasant villages, not too big or too small, which abounded in Germany. It had well-built homes in spacious gardens fully stocked with fruit and vegetables, with a few hens and geese to supplement the larder. The town was chosen because of its proximity to Lemgo the UNRRA zonal administration offices, to which I reported on the day after my arrival. It was with some trepidation that I entered the headquarters, a large building for so small a town, but my reception was surprisingly cordial. In fact, the UNRRA zone chief welcomed me like a long-lost friend. My previous contacts with the higher echelons had invariably been stormy. Now that I was part of the establishment I would be expected to conform, which would not be that easy. Control Commission was equally cordial and promised their assistance.

"The question of emigration to Palestine, or elsewhere was still the great bone of contention and the four hundred exit permits allowed made little impression on the increasing numbers."

I was introduced to a colonel whose special duties were the supervision of DP rehabilitation and re-education. He was an intelligent and discerning officer of much experience in the camps and his opinion was that the Jews in Belsen had not responded appropriately to the special aid and numerous relief workers in comparison with other camps. Many of his questions had a political slant and he was obviously interested to know how much I knew about the illegal emigration to Palestine.

It later transpired that this was his principal interest in Belsen. Some months later I had occasion to show a well-known London furniture manufacturer around the camp, who was willing to set up a small factory to teach the displaced persons how to make small articles of household furniture. He was to provide the machinery and the teaching staff if we could get permission to obtain the timber needed. I took the manufacturer along to see the colonel who turned down the proposition on the basis that sufficient was already being done and he felt that the project may result in an increase of the black market.

My first visit in the field had to be to Belsen, which I had not seen for some months. It was like going back into the firing line after a period of rest. There were many new faces, fresh arrivals that had infiltrated to fill the places of those who had moved on. The committee was obviously still maintaining its numbers.

All my Hungarian friends had departed, trekked back to their beloved Budapest, the artists, the footballers,

Life After Belsen

the athletes, probably led by Rudi the virtuoso, whose firm leadership they always followed. The 'lagerschwestern' (camp sisters) of Block B, a group of intelligent young girls who had stayed together since liberation had gone their different ways. Ilsa had left for Paris to continue her medical studies; Freda the raven-haired daughter of a Lithuanian professor had discovered some Australian cousins who had arranged for her transport; the Estonian blonde had married a Tommy and was now living in murky Manchester; and several of the others had joined the pilgrimage to Israel and were in transit in Cyprus.

But the central committee headed by Yossel was still there in full force. Yossel had been given quasi-official recognition as spokesperson for Jewish DPs in the British Zone, a tardy recognition of his power and his influence, but despite his elevation, he was still restricted to certain limits and his travelling was done with the aid and transport of the relief organisations. He would often turn up at Eilshausen at midnight, on some pretext or other, talk for a couple of hours and complete the ninety-mile return journey before dawn.

The vexed question of emigration to Palestine, or elsewhere for that matter, was still a bone of contention. The four hundred exit permits allowed under Operation Grand National made little impression on the ever-increasing numbers of displaced people looking to us for survival.

The search bureau of the International Red Cross was

still tracing and handing over Jewish children who had been hidden in Gentile homes. One of my first instructions from London was to provide an escort for a number of orphaned children found in Poland and brought by ship to Cuxhaven for transport to Britain. I appointed Alex for the assignment, a middle-aged Geordie from Newcastle-Upon-Tyne who was a real card. In civilian life he travelled Europe to record opera stars and as a sideline dealt in rare literary works. He was the odd job man of our unit, whose knowledge of Yiddish, combined with a literary turn of mind, may have been responsible for the pungent political articles that appeared in the Belsen camp magazine, 'Unser Sztime'.

"At Belsen DP camp there was none of the apathy, none of the hopelessness or feeling they were living on charity, that corrupter of morale, for all they received was only a small part of what was taken from them."

Alex's report back was amusing. He met his wards, about fifty of them, aboard the British ship which had brought them from Gydnia and was taking them on to Leith. Some of the 'children' had fully grown beards, and

Life After Belsen

all claimed to be Orthodox Jews, especially when there was any work or clearing up after meals to be done. Prayers instead of work was the golden rule! When Alex had shepherded his flock through customs and got them safely aboard the train for London, he found a bearded gentleman busily collecting wrist-watches from each of the children, certainly a novel way of evading the customs. Alex was furious and confiscated the smuggled timepieces, which he handed over to his relief in London.

My twelve months with the Jewish Relief Unit was the most hectic and exciting period of my three years on the Continent. It was the last phase of the struggle to liberate the thousands of Jews whose one desire was to go to Israel, the only country that offered them refuge without reservation of any kind. The successful conclusion of this mammoth task is a tribute to the courage and leadership of those who brought it about and to those in the camps who never gave up hope. Some of the events of that fateful year are told in the following chapter.

Chapter 17
In Search of a Normal Life
Kaunitz Camp, Germany

Over and above the Belsen Camp, which was bursting at the seams, the British Zone in Germany of 1946 had several thousand more displaced people who were scattered in smaller camps or hostels in Hanover, Lubeck, Hamburg, Dusseldorf and other places. These also came under the care of UNRRA and the special watch and ward of the Jewish Relief Organisations.

One such camp was at Kaunitz, a small village near Bielefeld in Westphalia about an hour's drive from the Jewish Relief Unit headquarters at Eilshausen. On my first visit to Kaunitz, I found a mixed group of Polish, Hungarian,

Life After Belsen

Romanian and Latvian Jews accommodated in German houses. These poor men and women were living in enforced idleness and seemed completely out of place in this rural setting and as they received a portion of their rations from German supplies they were not exactly popular with their neighbours.

The story of how the Kaunitz Camp started was told to me by Ella Rothauser, a young Hungarian Jewess, who was one of our typists at UNRRA headquarters in Eilshausen. During the war, she had been taken from her home near Budapest and incarcerated at the Auschwitz Extermination Camp, near Kraków in Poland, where the sign above the entrance gate proclaimed the false promise, 'Arbeit macht frei' (Work sets you free).

"They were living in wooden barracks and given the bare minimum to stay alive. Only those who've witnessed forced labour camps can imagine the dreadful conditions they had to endure."

If that wasn't horrific enough, in August 1944, she and several other young women were removed from the notorious camp and sent to work in a munitions factory in Lippstadt, a town not far from Bielefeld in Germany. The factory made spare parts for aeroplanes and tanks as well as hand grenades. About eight hundred Jewish women were employed there, two-thirds were Poles, the remainder Hungarians, and some Czechs. They worked twelve hours a day, alternating between day and night shifts. Their living quarters were the usual overcrowded wooden barracks and they were given the bare minimum amount of food necessary to keep them fit enough for work. Only those who have seen conditions in forced labour camps can imagine under what dreadful conditions these girls had to live.

Air raids by Allied planes were frequent and on the increase and these were welcomed by the girls as they brought the hope of liberation. Their Nazi jailers rushed for the bunkers during the raids, the concrete bombproof shelters so common in Germany, and weren't in a hurry to return. This gave the workers an opportunity to slip back to the barracks and rest until the 'all clear'. Moreover, the more frequent the raids, the greater the hope of freedom.

On 28 March, 1945 the women were suddenly ordered to gather their few belongings, a tattered blanket or ragged garment, because they were being marched to Belsen. One can imagine their consternation and terrible distress on hearing this news, which to them was a veritable death knell. They had heard about Belsen and knew this meant journey's end. The blow was all the more heartbreaking because they knew the Allied forces were getting closer and now their

Life After Belsen

hopes were dashed to the ground.

They were each issued with a loaf of rye bread and a piece of wurst and herded off like cattle. They moved only at night in the charge of a score of Schutzstaffel (SS) guards many of which were women. They were steered clear of main roads and had to trample through fields and woods and sleep during the day in barns, outhouses, and often in ditches. This was to keep them out of sight of the Allied planes that were scouring the skies looking for German columns. From snatches of conversation amongst the SS guards, the girls overheard that they were in the fighting zone and hoped against hope to be overtaken by the advancing troops.

It's difficult to imagine what this straggling multitude of women must have looked like, clothed in rags, some shod in wooden clogs, others barefoot, all with shaven heads covered by old blankets serving as a shawl or coat. On 1 April after a night in ditches, they heard the rattle of machine gun fire and their guards suddenly disappeared. The more adventurous girls had been foraging for sugar beet in the fields risking being shot by the guards. The girls noticed that white flags were flying from the windows of houses in the distance and heard the rumbling of heavy transport coming from the main road. Were they German tanks or was it the Allies?

Several of the girls crept up to the road and then stood up and began calling and waving hysterically, beckoning the others to come. The liberators had arrived. The Yanks had come at last. Ella could speak a little English and managed to explain to the advancing American troops who they were, why they were in rags and why their heads were shaven.

> *"They were being marched to Belsen which to them was a veritable death knell. They had heard about the horror camp and knew this meant journey's end. The blow was more heartbreaking because they knew the Allies were getting nearer."*

The response was immediate. Food, cigarettes, chocolates, and things they had not seen in years were instantly showered upon them, the first of Hitler's slaves that the spearhead troops had encountered. When the excitement had subsided, and a GI of Polish extraction had conveyed the main facts to one of his officers, the women were packed into trucks and taken to the nearest village, which happened to be Kaunitz. There they were given temporary accommodation in German houses. Most of the owners had fled, while others had gone into hiding. They had left everything behind, including cellars filled with the loot of Europe and overflowing with food and other provisions.

Ella and a companion were given a room to share and

Life After Belsen

she still remembers the joy of sleeping that night in a real bed with clean sheets. After all she had been through, having a bath and putting on a silk nightdress impacted her the most. It is these small details that leave an indelible impression on the memory, the sharpness of which is never eradicated.

By the time I visited Kaunitz many of the original girls had left, some had returned to Hungary and Czechoslovakia, others had gone to Canada, the USA, and Australia. The women who had stayed behind had married men from other camps and brought them to start a family in Kaunitz where many babies were born. A small Jewish community was now trying to live a normal life amongst alien surroundings while they hoped for safe passage to Israel. Those who were left were eagerly waiting for the day when they could shake off the bloodstained dust of Germany from their feet and start a new life in a free land, far away from this land of dreadful memories. Our heart's cry at the time was, "Please God, may it be soon."

On the day of my visit, there was much excitement as the first batch of exit permits under the Grand National operation had arrived, and twenty-seven lucky recipients were making preparations to go to the transit camp to join others on the journey to the Promised Land. That day the camp leader was so elated that he forgot to present his usual list of grievances. For a moment, all was well with the world.

Chapter 18
Other Jewish Camps
The American Zone

One of my first tasks at the Jewish Relief Unit was to visit our teams working in the camps and hostels in the American Zone. There were others in the Austrian camps but my trip to visit them would have to wait. As our administrative headquarters was at Eilshausen in the British Zone our workers in the other zones were seconded to the American Joint Distribution Committee with which we had a working arrangement.

The 'Joint' a worldwide Jewish relief organisation had hundreds of trained social workers and administrators in camps all over Europe, wherever there were Jewish refugees in need of help. The problem of dealing with Jewish displaced

Life After Belsen

persons in the US Zone, where the estimated number was half a million, was by virtue of its size alone, infinitely greater than in the British Zone.

The main stream of refugees that flooded out of the Iron Curtain countries in 1946 headed for the US Zone where they were treated as displaced persons and not as refugees, a distinction that carried several privileges. There were other important differences in the zonal administrations. The difficult question of emigration to Palestine was not harassed by politics as it was in the British Zone, where emigration was restricted to four hundred people a month. In fact, illegal immigration was unofficially assisted and there were many camps where youngsters were openly trained and prepared to run the British blockade.

"My most heartening impression of the US Zone was the activities of young people led by teachers of the Jewish Agency. These youngsters were the finest raw material that would help ensure the success of the new Jewish State."

On our visits to these special camps, our service uniform always provoked arguments about British policy. The Jewish People could never understand why Britain the creator of the national home for the Jews in Palestine should prevent them going there. Many of the senior UNRRA officials were American Jews who fully understood the problem and who realised early on that the only solution was a mass exodus to Palestine.

On Sunday, 1 June, in glorious weather, with Bernard Rawlings a British ex-sergeant as my guide, we set off from our headquarters at Eilshausen heading southeast for the American Zone. Travelling along the Autobahn, which goes right on to Austria, we passed Frankfurt before we left the main route and made for Lindenfels, our first port of call.

As we left the Autobahn we could see in the distance a 'Bismarck Tour' on the highest fell which so dominated the countryside that we were tempted to make for it and stop off and see the view. We did not think at the time that we would spend the night within a few hundred yards of this lookout. The car climbed steadily up the twisting road to Lindenfels and when we were halfway through this Medieval village we spotted two Polish Jews who answered our greeting of 'shalom' and directed us to the UNRRA team's headquarters.

The house was almost in the shadow of the 'Bismarck Tour' and had been built by a Swedish Jew as a summer resort just before the war, but he never had the good fortune to live in it. A bungalow structure of unusual design, with two sides at right angles that acted as a sun-trap, it provided exquisite views of the surrounding countryside.

Life After Belsen

We were welcomed by the UNRRA director, an American of French descent, who kept her team, fully occupied and seemed more concerned with her card index than the four hundred orphaned children and a hundred or so adults in her care. These were housed in the village, four hostels for the children and two for the adults, in buildings that before the war had served as holiday homes, equipped with modern kitchens and appliances and staffed by Germans.

What struck us most when we visited the hostels was the average size of the children who seemed to have stopped growing. Youngsters of fifteen were no taller than the average child of ten. They were some of the hundreds, perhaps thousands of children who had been hidden in Polish homes when their parents were taken away by the Nazis, and now through the efforts of the Jewish organisations and the International Red Cross, they were being cared for and prepared for their new home in Israel.

Our worker, a German Jewess, was perturbed about the insufficient supply of food for these ravenous children, who never seemed to have enough, and were making up for the lean years. The Israeli teacher who joined us was more concerned with their progress in Hebrew. "Once they get to Israel', he said, "Plenty of sun and good Jewish food will soon build up their bodies". We left the following morning with the promise that we would ask the benevolent Joint for special rations for our diminutive wards.

Simon Bloomberg

We soon began to realise the size of the problem. Camps were scattered all over Southeast Germany and Bavaria, varying in population from over five thousand to a few hundred. Some were like Belsen, modern barracks but others were decrepit huts in the former forced labour camps. They were bug-ridden and unsanitary hovels while the fortunate few lived in sanatoriums or hostels or in houses requisitioned from the Germans. The brightest spots were the 'Achshara'. These were farms set aside for the teaching of agriculture, where devoted Israeli instructors infused such enthusiasm into their pupils with untiring energy. At Hochlandlager three hundred healthy young men and women were running a mixed farm that produced both meat and milk and even the forbidden pork.

> *"They were all Jews and all had the one desire, to go to Palestine. The problem he said, could be solved overnight, and the solution was in the hands of the interrogators to 'Let My people go.'"*

Another such Achshara we visited later at Gersfield near Bamberg was run by a hundred or so youngsters bursting with good health and high spirits who showed us their cows,

Life After Belsen

calves, a prize bull, horses and a young filly, and then took us around the orchards and fields of corn. It happened to be Friday and that evening we all sat down to a traditional Sabbath meal.

A camp at Poking was a heartening example of what could be done to rehabilitate people, many of whom had been in concentration camps and forced labour camps for years. It was huge wooden barracks on the edge of a Luftwaffe airfield with over seven thousand people – Jews from Poland, Hungary, Romania and the Baltic states, all divided into their respective groups with their own representative on the camp committee. Here we saw the bearded Chassidim working on looms of their own construction, weaving cloth for use in a clothing factory that employed many workers. This clothing was then distributed in the DP camps by the Military Government. The camp even had an art school run by a Hungarian professor who begged us to obtain supplies for his many pupils.

> *"Apathy was a word unknown in the Jewish vocabulary. Their resilience was amazing. They seemed to be able to adapt to any circumstances and find a way to engage in gainful activities, working at their trades."*

Simon Bloomberg

The UNRRA director in charge of the camp, an engineer in civilian life, was busy building a swimming pool around a hot sulphur spring, found near the capo during oil boring operations. The whole camp was a hive of industry.

Landsberg was another such camp, where the people were housed in modern barracks, similar to Belsen. It was run by a strong central committee, strangely enough, most of them Latvians. A furniture factory was turning out small tables and plywood suitcases, the tailors, and shoemakers all working to capacity and the leather bar workers, who were Chassidim, trying to catch up with their orders. Landsberg had many teachers, volunteers from the Jewish Agency of Palestine, interested mainly in the hundreds of young people who were desperately anxious to emigrate to Israel. Our own worker had been there since August 1945, and her work was highly commended by the UNRRA director in charge.

Perhaps the most impressive effort at rehabilitation that we encountered on our trip was at Lampertheim near Mannheim, a solo effort by one of our workers, a cockney business woman, who had established a modern clothing factory complete with modern machinery employing about one hundred people making suits and other clothing. Betty had come to an arrangement with the local military officer to supply the machinery and cloth. The suits were returned to the Military Government for distribution in DP camps, and payment for the work was made in vouchers that could be

Life After Belsen

used to purchase amenities from a shop set up in the village. Betty's wards were fortunate enough to live in houses requisitioned from the Germans.

Our longest trip took us up to Hof right on the Czechoslovakian border about two hundred and fifty miles from Munich. Hof is a town famous for its crockery and fine glassware. It had not suffered from the ravages of war and was working overtime turning out cups and saucers for export. Much of its finer produce went into the US Cost Exchanges (canteens) to be snapped up and sent back to the USA. Hof had several DP camps, and was obviously a starting point for the trained 'Aliyahs', trying to run the blockade into Palestine.

The camp leader was a remarkable man who claimed to be the only displaced person to be appointed as a UNRRA director. He had been a sergeant serving with the British Army in the desert campaign and had finished up with the Jewish Brigade in Germany. After the cessation of hostilities, many of the soldiers in the Brigade had changed into civilian clothes and made their way behind the Iron Curtain hoping to find surviving relatives or friends and bring them back to the camps in Germany. Our host had been one of these travellers and had come back into Germany as a displaced person, and been posted to Hof to help the 'Aliyahs'.

His extraordinary talent for organisation probably attracted the attention of UNRRA and resulted in his appointment. The ex-sergeant seemed to run the town. He showed us a chinaware factory where he certainly had much to do with its success. He had a great sense of humour and his ability to manage people was an education in how to meet all situations from cajoling an exasperated kindergarten teacher to showing a ten-year-old boy how to make a football out of rags. The most heartening impressions of my trip to the US Zone were the activities of the younger groups in the camps, under the leadership of the teachers of the Jewish Agency for Palestine. Here was the finest material that would help to ensure the success of the new Jewish state. For these youngsters, there was only one destination and nothing would stop them getting there.

> *"The Jewish People could never understand why Britain, the creator of the national home for Jews, should prevent them from going there. The only solution was a mass exodus."*

The kibbutzim were the shock troops of the future, boys and girls, self-disciplined, eager to absorb knowledge, living a communal way of life which abjured the materialism of the Western world. Not that there was any apathy among the older group; apathy was a word unknown in the Jewish vocabulary. The resilience of these people was amazing, they

Life After Belsen

seemed to be able to adapt themselves to any circumstances and find a way to engage in gainful activities, working at their trades as craftsmen, or in 'gesheft', petty trading, sometimes not strictly regular in the eyes of the law. It was jocularly said that some of them could go out of camp with a pair of shoelaces and come back with a pair of shoes.

During our trip Ben and I covered some three thousand miles travelling from the northern extremities of the US Zone to the border of Austria and back to the Czech border and back north to the British Zone. We witnessed the plight of about one hundred and forty-five thousand Jewish DPs scattered over this vast area. Some lived in reasonably good conditions, in houses or hostels, some in barracks formerly used by German troops, but the vast majority were still cramped together in the labour camps where Hitler caged his foreign slaves.

Chapter 19
A New Jewish Refugee Crisis
Vienna, Austria

By midsummer of 1947 UNRRA was being phased out, giving way to the International Refugee Organisation (IRO). However, the takeover had hardly changed the personnel, except most of the more capable UNRRA officers had left and returned to their civil vocations and there had been a weeding out of the rest. Fortunately, I had pre-empted this with my protest resignation while being able to remain at the centre of the ongoing crisis, where I hoped to make a meaningful difference.

The aim of the new organisation was a rapid dissolution of the DP and refugee population through repatriation and

Life After Belsen

emigration. The hard core that could not, or would not move, was to be absorbed into the local economy.

The Jews were considered 'a special problem', which had increased over the past year by the enormous increase of refugees from countries behind the Iron Curtain, especially Romania. The few possibilities of emigration to the Americas and other countries and the small quotas to Palestine had made no dent on the growing numbers. The main factor was the desire of most of the people to go to Israel, they rarely, if ever, spoke of it as Palestine. In June and July, a new surge of Jewish refugees swept into the US Zones of Germany and Austria and old and abandoned camps had to be reopened. In the small enclave that was now Austria, the influx was a severe embarrassment to the harassed economy. The relief organisations were working at full strength using up their reserve supplies in an endeavour to deal with the crisis.

"A new surge of Jewish refugees swept into Germany and Austria and old camps had to be reopened, with the relief organisations working at full strength to deal with the crisis."

In Vienna itself, over seven thousand refugees, mainly

from Romania were crowded into three camps, half of them into the famous Rothschild Hospital. The desperate scenes there beggared belief. The recreation rooms, passages, cellars, even the lavatories were overcrowded with people lying about, some on improvised beds, others on the bare floor. The outside courtyards were full of jostling crowds, some of which had just arrived as we were there, and were being medically examined before registration. The administration, working around the clock, had broken down under the strain.

I spoke to many new arrivals, some of which were reasonably dressed, but in the main, they were poorly clad. All were in bad shape physically particularly the children who looked like famine cases. Babies with suppurating sores were lying half naked on the floor with distracted mothers trying to keep the flies off their little, wasted bodies. One mother stripped the coats off her two diminutive wide-eyed boys to substantiate her harrowing pleas. The whole building stank of wretched humanity in the last stages of exhaustion.

Only an artist like the British satirist, William Hogarth could have depicted these scenes of despair – an old woman in gaudy colours squatting on the bed of a sick woman turning over cards and whispering what they foretold. Fat well-fed spivs moving among the crowds looking for jewellery and other bargains, like vultures picking the bones of their dying victims and a pale-faced, aesthetic looking man sitting near his sick wife playing soothing music on his violin.

Life After Belsen

Fortunately, the Joint was able to produce food from its reserve stocks to feed the newcomers until other sources became available and the Russians were, for a change, cooperative by allowing the refugees to go through the Russian Zone to the camps in the US Zone of Germany. None of the refugees I spoke to could give any definite evidence of persecution, but mass hysteria and the fear of famine and possibly political propaganda had started the flight, which had grown into a panic fearful enough to make them leave their homes and all their belongings.

There was little we could do until additional staff and supplies arrived and as it happened to be the August bank holiday weekend, with all the official offices closed and our contacts away fishing or holidaying in the surrounding countryside, I decided to visit a Jewish camp at Admont in the British Zone about a hundred and fifty miles south of Vienna.

Bernard, my driver looked at his map and decided to take a short cut across the country via Lunz, on a secondary road that would take miles off the journey. Vienna, like Berlin, was an island in the Russian Zone. Access to which required special passes grudgingly issued by the Russian authorities. A grey pass had been issued to us at Linz when we entered the zone.

We left the Rothschild Hospital about three in the afternoon hoping to reach our destination before nightfall. Winding our way along a river valley between the mountains we passed many small villages where we hoped to buy some fruit, a vain hope because the countryside seemed to have been gleaned of everything edible. There were very few signs of the Russian occupation, only at one small village did we see a banner with a hammer and sickle hung up across the main street, but we saw no Russian troops until we were almost through the zone when we were held up by a wooden barrier across the road.

> *"Mass hysteria and the fear of famine and possibly political propaganda had started the flight which had grown into a panic fearful enough to make them leave their homes and all their belongings."*

The guards tumbled out of a nearby hut, a motley crowd of unwashed, unshaven soldiers some in their bare feet and all carrying guns. One of them inspected our grey pass and tried to read it upside down. He didn't seem to be able to understand us and another ran off to call the officer in charge. A pimply-faced young lieutenant appeared who spoke a little German. He listened patiently to what we had to say and inspected our other papers.

We told him that we were relief officers in British military uniform and our destination was a DP camp in the

Life After Belsen

British Zone. When we thought we had convinced him of the bona fides of our journey he suddenly ordered two of his armed men into the back of our car and told us to go back along the road to another post where there was a more senior officer. So back we went for about twenty miles, pulling up at a house where one of our guards got out and returned to the car giving us signs to carry on still further along the road.

Our next stop was outside an inn where a dance was in progress and after a while, two officers emerged, one a young artillery captain and the other an elderly soldier. Once again, we repeated our story, showing our pass and papers. I was invited inside the inn while Bernard and the two guards sat in the car outside. When we sat down at a small table on the edge of the dance floor, the younger of the two officers banged on the table and barked at a passing waiter. "Vodka schnell" was his command, sending the waiter scurrying off to return quickly with the drinks which were consumed in the usual Russian fashion.

More drinks were ordered and I sat sipping my third while the younger officer went off to dance with one of the village maidens. When he returned I ventured to suggest that all was well and that we could continue on our journey, to which the officer replied, "I have arranged for you to be taken to the commandant for identification". When I protested I was informed that I was now in the Russian Zone and would do as I was told. Our guard was changed and off we went into the gathering darkness with two young soldiers who were not sure of the way. One of them spoke a little Auslander Deutsch and kept stopping the car to get directions.

It was nearing midnight when we pulled up at a railway junction and after what seemed an interminable wait, a dour looking official flashed a torchlight on us and asked his interpreter to question us. Once again, our story was told, and once again we produced our papers. He was obviously a person of high rank and I gathered from snatches of his conversation with the interpreter that he wasn't satisfied with our story.

A year's close contact with a Ukrainian camp had taught me a smattering of Russian and I heard the word 'spy' being bandied about. We were told we would be under guard until the morning, when our identity could be established. I protested strongly and asked to be allowed to ring up the Control Commission in Vienna. I also produced my notebook with the names and phone numbers of the officers I wished to contact in Vienna. The mention of Colonel Logan Grey must have struck a chord because, after a further consultation with his interpreter, I was informed that permission was granted for us to get back on to the main road and return at once to Vienna. At about three o'clock in the morning we fled from the Russian outpost praying that we could find our way to the main road without being stopped again.

Just as daylight was breaking we reached Vienna, tired,

Life After Belsen

dirty, hungry and fed up to the teeth. On the Tuesday after the Bank Holiday, we related our story to Control Commission and were told we were very lucky because only a few days before a Swiss Red Cross car had been fired upon and one of the occupants killed. Never again did Bernard try a short cut!

Later in the week, we left for Admont, this time making sure that all our papers were in order, and that we had the correct route. On the first part of the journey, across the flat lands, the temperature was in the nineties and hot winds like the turning blasts of the Sudan blew dust devils along the roads. Climbing up the hairpin bends into the mountains after leaving Bruck the air became cooler and fragrant and by the evening we were running along a pleasant river valley, which led to Admont.

"In Vienna the desperate scenes beggared belief – people lying on improvised beds, others on the floor. The whole building stank of wretched humanity in the last stages of exhaustion."

At the road barrier which marked the end of the Russian Zone a massive picture of Stalin surmounted a high flagpole, the picture facing the British post, and four hundred yards further along after a stretch of 'no man's land' we reached the

Simon Bloomberg

British barrier, where a picture of George VI with a Union Jack flying above the King's head faced the Russian Zone. We arrived at the camp about seven o'clock in the evening to be welcomed by the director, a pleasant easy-going ex-UNRRA man who seemed popular with his heterogeneous wards, Jews from all the countries behind the Iron Curtain.

After Vienna and the Rothschild Hospital, Admont was a haven of peace. That evening the camp was celebrating the official supply of uniforms to its camp police, any excuse for a celebration, and we were among the honoured guests. The camp orchestra started off by playing the British national anthem, 'God Save the King' followed by the 'Hatikvah' the Israeli anthem, both sung vociferously by all.

Then the dancing commenced and while the energetic 'Hora' dancers were hurling themselves around in a ring we crept away quietly to our beds. The following day we left for Salzburg through wild precipitous mountain country and along beautiful valleys reaching our destination without any further trouble from our Russian allies.

It was early November when we next visited Vienna, this time for a Conference of Chiefs of the IRO and Control Commission, to discuss the future role of the voluntary societies in what we hoped was to be the winding up of the DP and refugee crisis. On our arrival at Salzburg, we had to get permission from the US Army to visit the camps and our reception was not exactly friendly.

Life After Belsen

The young colonel who kept us waiting for most of the morning started a quick-fire interrogation, with "Who are you? Why have you come? And, do you have clearance to enter the zone". When we produced our papers, he volunteered his opposing views on 'the Jewish question' saying he admired Great Britain's policy over Palestine and deplored any attempts at illegal immigration. He asked suspiciously whether we were members of the Haganah and if the Jews would be able to defend themselves if the British withdrew. He rapped out his questions like a sergeant major addressing rookies on parade. Finally, with obvious reluctance, he gave us the necessary permission and instructed us to report to a US colonel in Vienna.

In and around Salzburg there were many camps and hostels, several of them Jewish, and in the pleasant lake country a few miles away there were orphanages for the hundreds of children whose parents had been liquidated by the Nazis. One of these was run by a young married couple from Leeds, both teachers, whose idealism had prompted them to start their married life as voluntary relief workers. They were ideal foster parents for their wards and ran their orphanage like a well-conducted boarding school.

We had stayed there before, on a previous visit, and the children crowded around asking many questions about where we had been in the interim period. One youngster, a chess prodigy, insisted on repeating his victories and nailed me down to three games all of which he won in record time.

A Canadian commission had just visited the home and was arranging to take some of the children to Canada, to be settled in homes of people willing to adopt them. It was during the school holidays, but there was a plan for tuition and recreation each day and after breakfast I sat on a bench under a large beech tree listening to a story of recent happenings in Palestine, related in Yiddish, by a teacher from the Jewish Agency of Palestine. I was, as usual, put in the position of the defending counsel and my strong point was as always that the national home for Jews could never have come about, but for Great Britain.

It was some time after reaching Vienna that we learned that the young couple from Leeds were in trouble. They had been sent out from our London headquarters by an unusual route and had not been informed about currency restrictions in Austria. The Englishman had a few pounds, the legal allowance, but this was not acceptable in the US canteens. He managed to exchange the Sterling but unfortunately, the dollar bills he was given were forgeries and were traced back to him. The unsuspecting gentleman from Leeds was then summoned before a US court.

As a director of the unit, it was incumbent on me to do what I could to help the unfortunate young man, so I returned to Salzburg, arranged for a defending counsel and asked to be allowed to testify as to the good character of the accused.

Life After Belsen

The informality of the court with an American judge in civilian clothes smoking a cigar was like a scene out of a Hollywood film. I sat down alongside an interpreter and a stenographer and the accused, looking frightened, was seated near a US military policeman. After the oath was administered I testified that the couple had been sent out in a hurry from England without being properly briefed by our headquarters. The judge, after making disparaging remarks about the inefficiency of the Jewish Relief Unit staff gave the defendant the benefit of the doubt, and after a reprimand, dismissed the case.

Back in Vienna, things had improved. Most of the refugees had been sent to camps in the Salzburg and Munich area and the Rothschild Hospital had resumed its normal functions. We were shown around by a competent woman doctor, a Viennese, and we spoke to many of the patients, some of which had been at Auschwitz. They had been repatriated to Romania, did not want to stay there and were now hoping to go to Palestine.

One patriarch of some sixty odd years spoke excellent French, he had lived in France for many years, was hoping to get back there, where he had a brother. His one treasured possession was a coloured plaque of Léon Blum the Jewish French politician, a talisman he had carried about for years.

The return journey was not free from incident. On reaching Linz through which we had passed a few days

Simon Bloomberg

previously, we were held up by the Russian guard who told us that according to the Yalta Agreement only French and American personnel could pass that way. When told that we had used the route before, he was unmoved, but after much argument he allowed me to walk over the bridge to consult with the US military police, holding on to our passes as security for my return. I explained our predicament to the GI guard, who rang up his officer, telling him two 'Limeys' had been stopped by the 'Russkies', and wanted his advice. The advice given was to go on talking until they let us through. We acted on this advice but the Russians were adamant and when they threatened to arrest us and impound the car we decided to return to Vienna.

> *"What hopes had these people for the future, where could they go? My sympathies were naturally with those who tried to leave Germany. How could they be otherwise? But, I also believed the national home for Jews couldn't have come about, but for Great Britain."*

To add to our troubles, we ran out of petrol and had to be towed for the last fifteen miles. We were told that the grey passes had just been changed, but that in any case we would

Life After Belsen

be well advised to return to the British Zone via Semmering, the route authorised for British personnel. We got a couple more stamps on our passes just to impress the Russians and set off via Semmering, Bruck, and Leoban following the Valley of the Inn through miles of snow-capped peaks and scenic countryside.

When we finally got to the correct crossing point the Russian guard didn't ask any questions. He tried to read the passes sideways, took them into his sentry box and kept us waiting for ten anxious minutes before returning the passes and lifting the barrier. We cheered when we saw the 'Jack' flying proudly at the other end of the bridge, where we were greeted by a friendly Tommy who told us we could get a good cup of 'Cha' at Bruck.

Chapter 20
Back Behind Barbed Wire
The Exodus

It was mid-August, shortly after my return to Belsen from Austria that the plight of the Jewish ship, 'The Exodus' became front-page news in the world media. Before the story broke we gathered something important was happening from the number of secret meetings at Belsen between the Central Jewish Committee, the Jewish Agency for Palestine and the American Joint Distribution Committee, to which I was not invited. As a British relief unit we carefully steered clear of politics and although we knew that illegal immigration into Palestine was being stepped up, it was with us a case of 'Nelson's blind eye'.

Life After Belsen

We knew that a travelling synagogue presented to Belsen by the Council of Rabbis made long journeys southwards and was away on its spiritual safaris for a week at a time. The 'Ark of the Covenant' was a roomy vehicle that could carry many worshippers. The sole topic of conversation was the story of the interception of the blockade runner with its four thousand plus Jews within sight of 'Eretz Yisrael' and their forcible transfer to three steamers with the intention of returning them to France where they had originally embarked. It was only later that we learned that The Exodus, an old cargo ship had been bought in the States and sent to Marseilles to pick up its passengers who had been assembled there from different parts of Europe, and that the scheme was a desperate attempt to force Britain's hand to open the gates of Palestine to the thousands of Jewish refugees who were adamant to make aliyah.

"We were caught between dual loyalties, being a British unit yet working for a solution to the Jewish refugee situation, that could only be solved by the emigration of the vast majority."

Tragically more than four thousand Jewish political pawns had been refused landing and were forced to turn

Simon Bloomberg

back to Europe. They were returned to France where they refused to disembark at Marseilles and it was decided to send them to Germany – a move that played right into the hands of Israeli sympathisers and their American friends. And of course, the new German administration was aghast at the idea of putting Jewish People back into camps behind barbed wire, in notorious hovels that had so recently been used as concentration camps.

On 23 August 1947, the Jewish Relief Unit was told we would be expected to help when the refugees landed at Hamburg to which we agreed on the condition that we would not be expected to take part in the disembarkation, which we thought might be forcibly resisted.

We were caught in the cleft stick of dual loyalties, a British organisation subsidised like other British voluntary relief societies by the Foreign Office, yet at the same time we were working on a solution to the Jewish refugee problem in Europe, which we knew could only be solved by the emigration of the vast majority to Palestine, the only country willing to accept them. The other two Jewish relief organisations we worked with, in close cooperation, the one from the USA and the other from Palestine had no such problem and were in fact, openly opposed to British policy. When our decision to go in and help became known we received an urgent summons to attend a meeting a Belsen called by the Central Jewish Committee, a meeting that had

Life After Belsen

apparently been going on non-stop for a couple of days. The committee had just taken over 'The Rundhause', the one-time officers' mess of the Nazi Panzer Regiment, a palatial building by military standards and President Yossel and his Presidium were installed in the large conference room around a massive table which was part of the original furniture.

We received a frigid reception. The usual friendly address of chaverim (comrades) was noticeably absent from the tirade of questions they shot at us. Why had we promised to help at Hamburg? Did we not know we were betraying the cause by promising collaboration with the enemy?

One after the other they protested against us, some with hostility: Kurt of the Jewish Agency for Palestine; Hadassah Rosensaft, the president's wife and mentor; Norman a German Jewish leader and survivor of concentration camps and even Vida, my friend from the American Joint. We were well and truly in the doghouse.

As the director of the unit I promised to inform our London headquarters of the discussions at the meeting. The chairman of our German section was at that moment trying to persuade the authorities to divert the three transports to Britain but I knew this would be refused.

Meanwhile, we were being pressed to submit plans to Control Commission for our provision of help at Hamburg to assist with the disembarkation of the survivors of The Exodus, and on 4 September an ultimatum was received from a colonel at control headquarters, giving us until noon to make up our minds. So, the pressure was on from all sides.

Relief came just before zero hour in the form of a request from the IRO to attend a meeting at their headquarters presided over by General Fanshawe, chief of the British Zone, who had just returned from Geneva where The Exodus incident had been discussed. The other Jewish voluntary societies were also present and the general appealed to us to go in on humanitarian grounds and help our kinsmen. When asked about IRO's attitude in the matter, he replied that it had been instructed to help, provided no force was used at the disembarkation.

> *"Even the Germans were aghast at the idea of putting the refugees back into camps behind barbed wire, camps so recently used as concentration camps."*

Finally, it was agreed to send a joint medical unit to stand by and render assistance if necessary. Many journalists had already invaded Hamburg, the majority from the USA, all hoping for sensational stories. The docks had been cordoned off and only two representative pressmen were allowed to go on board when the three vessels came into the harbour.

A fog delayed the first landing and a spare day faced the newsmen with little to do, so a visit to Belsen was arranged

Life After Belsen

for them and down they came with their cameras. A couple of thousand people milled around amongst the rabbis to hear several speakers, including Yossel who was on top form, passionately sharing the plight of the Jewish survivors of the Holocaust and their right to return to Eretz Yisrael. Somebody in the crowd had hoisted a Union Jack, at which fists were shaken while the camera clicked, but Yossel boldly sprang from his rostrum and rebuked the offenders and the cameramen. After this we all trooped back to Hamburg, about ninety miles away, the journey enlivened by the anti-British views of our two journalist passengers one a young American from *The Denver Post*. When we countered by asking what

"Like Pharaoh, the Foreign Office still refused to let the Children of Israel go and feelings in the camps became embittered and for the British relief workers, it was hard to justify this policy."

specific aid the USA had provided in the matter of immigration the surprised reply was "I thought you were on our side?"

Accommodation in Hamburg was almost non-existent. The RAF raids had left the city a heap of rubble, civilian casualties were estimated to have been as high as a quarter of a million and black crosses were painted on many of the huge mounds of rubble where victims of the raids still lay buried. Only two hotels, the Atlanta and the Reichshof had escaped serious damage and both had been requisitioned by Control Commission the former as an officers' club and the latter to accommodate VIPs and visiting personnel.

The Atlanta Hotel was full of military and Control Commission officers, awaiting the outcome of the disembarkation of all those who had been on board The Exodus and there were all kinds of rumours flying around about what action would be taken against the Jewish relief organisations for their refusal to help. One British newspaper came out with a report that we were to be expelled from the zone as a punishment for our non-cooperation.

The first of the three ships to berth was the Ocean Vigour, occupied mostly by women and children. The women and some four hundred children disembarked with little resistance but they disdainfully refused any help or comfort from the British Red Cross team on the quayside, demonstrating by their remarks and actions their bold stand for what they believed was right.

When the people of the second transport came off singing, having, so it was said, placed a homemade time bomb in the hold, General Fanshawe and the colonel acting as a special observer, made jesting remarks about the fears I had expressed of violent resistance.

However, the third vessel to arrive brought with it a

Life After Belsen

battle. The resisters refused to disembark and eventually had to be flushed out of the ship's holds with torrents of water from its hoses. Even then, the brave Jewish men fought back and had to be frog-marched down the gangways kicking and struggling. They put up a terrific fight.

That night the Atlanta Lounge was crowded with noisy newspapermen and women who had witnessed the battle between the British boarding party and the resisters from behind the dock barriers. The journalists were swapping stories of the battle, with the usual exaggerations and I heard one raven-haired, glamorous type, with painted face and dark glasses, describe vividly how she had seen a Jewess kick a soldier in what she described as 'his vulnerable parts'. Despite the rough handling, there were, fortunately, no serious injuries and the refugees were driven away to camps somewhere in the north.

During the disembarkations I spoke to several mysterious young men who appeared from nowhere and had apparently been on the transports. They must have come ashore while the ships were anchored and awaiting berthing. Two were avowed members of the Haganah and had contacts in Hamburg the other a young American Jew claimed he had crossed the Atlantic from Baltimore on the Warfield, which became The Exodus on its arrival in Marseilles. He had joined the refugees, continued the journey and described how the Exodus was rammed at night by British destroyers without lights, within sight of the coast of Palestine. To substantiate his account of what had happened, he produced a pamphlet dropped by the British on the ship in which a promise was made to take the refugees to Cyprus. He said that he had asked the American Relief organisation in Hamburg for help, but they refused to assist him. As he did not seem unduly perturbed at being in a restricted zone without papers or funds I gave him a little money and a supply of cigarettes and let him take care of himself.

> *"The Exodus affair must have influenced the British to give up their mandate on Palestine, withdrawing their troops and leaving the Jews and Arabs to settle their differences about partition on their own."*

Now that the battle was over an appeal was made to the military chief of the DP division to permit the relief organisations to go into the camps, where the people from The Exodus had been taken, but MI5 was too busy interrogating their victims to be interrupted by our solicitations to help. The search for members of the Haganah went on for days, but without any success, as every one of the refugees claimed to be lawful citizens of the State of Israel.

Life After Belsen

Finally, after much persuasion and as the Jewish holidays were approaching it was agreed one representative from each of the three relief agencies would be allowed to visit the camps. This was a special concession to meet the most urgent requirements while taking supplies for Rosh Hashanah and Yom Kippur (Day of Atonement). Other visitors were not encouraged and it was not until some weeks later that I was able to make a tour of the camps

The first was at Am Stau just beyond Travawunde not far from the Russian Zone boundary on the Baltic coast, where behind barbed wire, with military police guarding the gates, we met the camp leader who introduced himself as 'Anselm', since real names were not disclosed. He was a well-built young man who spoke perfect English and offered to show an attendant doctor and I around the camp. He asked if we would like to meet the British contingent. When we answered in the affirmative he took us to a hut where a dozen or so bright

"Living with displaced people was a sort of Kafka-like experience at times leading nowhere, that had warped my judgement to the extent I sometimes felt I'd become more displaced than my wards."

youngsters of the undergraduate type were housed. They politely refused offers to communicate with their supporters, perhaps to protect their identity and their only desire was reading matter, current literature and newspapers. They were anxious to know if there were any political repercussions to The Exodus incident but gave no indication of how they had been involved.

Camp conditions were appalling, broken-down wooden huts, the usual primitive sanitary arrangements, and to add to the misery it was pouring down with rain and there was mud everywhere. Despite this, there was no grumbling or complaints, the concern was mainly for the children and the sick. Our unit doctor was given a list of the sick to be examined and the worst cases were sent to the Glyn Hughes Hospital at Belsen.

At the second camp, Poppendorf, we caught up with the acknowledged leader of The Exodus, the one person identified by full name, Mordechai Rosman, a thin young man who spoke in rapid Yiddish in the same manner as Belsen camp leader, Yossel. He gave himself no airs and had no special mannerisms but he was reputed to be a man of steel. The fight he put up, against all odds, to resist disembarkation certainly proved his physical courage. He showed us around the camp, at the same time discussing the political position and the possible future of his followers. With him, I noticed the curly haired youngster I met in Hamburg who claimed

Life After Belsen

to have slipped over the side of the ship in the darkness and swum ashore.

Hut Thirty-One with nineteen newborn babies plus about twenty adults was the worst. Cots alongside beds, not a foot to spare between them, and a dining bench down the centre of the hut. It was reminiscent of the Rothschild Hospital in Vienna during the flight of the refugees from Romania. The heartening feature was the cheerfulness of the many youngsters to whom it was all one great adventure.

Some weeks later when 'intelligence' had vetted both camps, obviously without much success, the people were removed to other camps, desolate, forsaken places near the north coast. Sengwarden, a bleak outlandish district in the middle of nowhere, where the stone barracks were reminiscent of an old English workhouse, long sloping roofs, tiny windows and dull red brick walls. The buildings widely spaced apart left plenty of room for the North Sea winds to blast.

It was a veritable home for lost and deserted souls. There were incarcerated men and five hundred children, still as chirpy as ever, intent on keeping alive the spirit of The Exodus. The Agency teachers, those dedicated men, and women from Israel were, like their forebears, trying to make bricks without straw. No paper, no pencils, very few books or other essential supplies, but what was lacking in materials was made up for in enthusiasm. The school was held in the

Simon Bloomberg

upper rooms, dimly lit attics, and in the class, I sat through a lesson taught by a chubby-faced Israeli woman who was using a homemade blackboard, with the children straining to read the Hebrew words she was writing. Handing on the torch of education under such conditions of adversity was a challenge only the stoutest of hearts could have achieved.

"The declaration of the 'State of Israel' and its admission to the UN gave the Jews in the camps fresh hope of their early release from their bondage. Thousands from all over Europe headed towards the Promised Land."

As history shows, Jews throughout the ages have often been condemned to make bricks without straw and somehow, they have succeeded. Here they were making foundation stones by training young Jews to help build their new homeland. Only the strongest can work under such conditions of adversity and still carry on. That night there was a Hanukkah (Festival of Lights) celebration in the main building, where the camp police band, a saxophone, and a concertina, murdered 'The Blue Danube' waltz, the only tune they appeared to know. Bottles of home brewed liquor appeared from nowhere and the toast was 'L'Chaim' (to life).

Life After Belsen

The next day we went to the second camp, a place near Emden in windswept treeless countryside open to the gales of the North Sea. The buildings were better than those of Sengwarden, but they were pervaded by the same smell and atmosphere, that hangs over all refugee camps. At Emden, the spirit of The Exodus was very much alive in the people in the camp committees and in the relief workers. Our unit's doctor an Egyptian Jew, who had served with the British Army, was in excellent fettle, radiating his cheerfulness amongst his staff and patients. The Exodus leader, Rosman, was away in Munich, no doubt arranging for a further flight from the land, that held so many tragic memories for so many Jewish people, and it was his deputy who conducted us around.

"My time with the Jewish Relief Unit was the last phase in the struggle to liberate thousands of Jews. The successful conclusion of this task is a tribute to the courage of those who brought it about and those in the camps who never gave up."

He praised the atmosphere of the camp, said that there was no black market and that all supplies received were distributed fairly. Plans were afoot to give the youngsters a holiday in one of the convalescent camps in the Harz mountains from which they would probably be quietly removed to more amenable children's homes in the US Zone, ready for their next attempt at reaching Israel.

For all the displaced persons in liberated Europe, the beginning of 1948 held out few prospects of relief from their suffering. For the Jews, it seemed hopeless. The several commissions sent to Palestine to try and get the Arabs and the Jews to agree on some form of co-existence failed to find a solution acceptable to both parties.

Eventually it seemed that partition was the only way forward but there was no agreement. The possibility of considerable numbers of Jews emigrating to the United States under the projected 'Stratton Bill' raised the hopes of many, especially the middle aged and elderly who preferred the state-aided American scheme to the harsh conditions they knew they would face in the Promised Land.

The American Jewish Immigration Agency, which did excellent work placing so many displaced persons in different parts of the world, was far from popular with its Israeli counterpart, which fought tooth and nail against any schemes that sent Jews to any country, other than Palestine.

Some of the acts of the Jews who had been able to relocate to Palestine did not improve the situation for those in Europe rather they seemed to have had a Pharaoh-like effect on the British Foreign Office which still refused to

Life After Belsen

let the Children of Israel go. Feelings in the camps became embittered and for the British relief workers, it was difficult to justify His Majesty's Government's policy. The old problem of dual loyalties plagued the conscience of those loyal to the country of their birth, yet fully in sympathy with their unfortunate wards. The Exodus affair had shown how such an emotionally charged situation could affect one's judgement and decisions.

After three years of living with displaced people, one was apt to become more displaced than one's wards and I felt I couldn't achieve anything further. I personally couldn't see an early solution to the complex problem I considered would drag on for years to come. A fortuitous offer of re-employment in the Colonial Service provided the excuse if one was needed and I submitted my resignation, leaving Germany for good in February 1948, with a heavy heart. "My only regret is that I cannot stay on and see the general exodus of the Jews which I hope will start soon," I wrote to Leonard Cohen, the chairman of the Jewish Committee for Relief Abroad.

A month later I was in the office of the Crown Agents in London who look after the affairs of overseas officials, chatting with a South African who volunteered the information that he was a former Palestinian policeman, recently retired because the 'Stern gang' (freedom fighters opposed to the British Mandate in Palestine) were after his blood. When I asked him what he thought was going to happen he replied with much conviction, "The British are going to pull out within the next few months and leave the Jews to be driven into the sea by the Arabs." Fortunately, the first part of his forecast was correct, but thankfully his second prediction was completely wrong.

'The Exodus Affair' and its far-reaching political repercussions must have influenced the British Government to finally give up its mandate on Palestine, withdrawing its troops and leaving the Jews and Arabs to settle their differences about partition on their own.

The Declaration of the State of Israel and its admission to the United Nations gave the Jews in the camps fresh hope of their early release from bondage. Ultimately thousands from all over Europe headed towards the Promised Land. Many of them to join the Israeli forces against the Arab armies in the War of Independence. The oft-quoted ancient wish from the Passover Seder, "le-shanah ha-ba'ah bi-Yerushalayim," had finally come true – "Next Year in Jerusalem!"

Life After Belsen

You will arise and have compassion on Zion,
for it is time to show favour to her;
the appointed time has come...

For the Lord will rebuild Zion
and appear in His glory.
He will respond to the prayer of the destitute;
He will not despise their plea...

Let this be written for a future generation,
that a people not yet created may praise the Lord:

"The Lord looked down from his sanctuary on high,
from Heaven He viewed the earth,
to hear the groans of the prisoners
and release those condemned to death."

So the name of the Lord will be declared in Zion
and His praise in Jerusalem
when the peoples and the kingdoms
assemble to worship the Lord.

(Psalm 102:13-22)

Afterword

A Life of Service
by Al Gibson
Bloomberg, a Brief Biography

Jewish humanitarian and British colonial leader, Simon Bloomberg was born in Liverpool, England on 11 September 1894. He was the son of Lazarus Bloomberg and his wife Annie (nee Benjamin) whose family had to flee Russia to escape anti-Semitic riots. They lived at 42 Pellew Street (now demolished) and spent periods in New York where Simon received his first schooling. He had a good memory and could recite parts of the Gettysburg Address in First Grade.

Life After Belsen

"Four score and seven years ago our fathers brought forth on this continent, a new nation, conceived in liberty, and dedicated to the proposition that all men are created equal... we here highly resolve that these dead shall not have died in vain – that this nation, under God, shall have a new birth of freedom – and that Government of the people, by the people, for the people, shall not perish from the earth."

The address must have made a huge impact on Simon as a young lad as it was to this kind of equality that he aspired his whole life. He never showed any class superiority and would stop to talk to people of all walks of life.

His father, Lazarus was a pioneer in the Trade Union movement in Liverpool who helped to secure workers' rights. He set up health insurance for the Jewish community, through the care of immigrant doctors fleeing the pogroms. Simon longed to be a doctor like his father's business associates but due to family commitments had to give up a scholarship to Oxford and instead he started working at an early age.

Having left school, he joined the Civil Service as a boy clerk. However, he continued to study at night school where he won various book prizes including Collected Works of Wordsworth and Shakespeare. His work with the Civil Service took him to the Home Office in London where

Simon Bloomberg

Winston Churchill was Home Secretary from 1910-1911. He also served in Manchester and at the Custom House in Liverpool. He wanted to fight in World War I but had to wait until he was released by the Civil Service. He enlisted in the British Army on 1 December 1915 at twenty-one. His soldier's pay book lists him as a signaller and his religion is given as 'Hebrew'. Simon served in France and Flanders (Belgium) and became a gunner with the Royal Horse Artillery, caring for the horses that pulled the guns. He fought in some of the worst battles, saw the trenches where so many bodies were left lying in the mud and never forgot his fellow servicemen who didn't return home. He was the victim of mustard gas near the end of the war and received a war pension for five years.

> *"Simon dived into the river to rescue him, an heroic act that was recorded in the local newspaper an early indication of the benevolence and humanitarianism that would define his life."*

After the war, Simon went back to Customs and Exercise in Liverpool. One day he was crossing the River Mersey on a ferry when a boy fell overboard. Simon dived in to rescue him, a heroic act that was recorded in the local newspaper and an early indication of the benevolence and

Life After Belsen

humanitarianism that would define his life.

Simon was a keen golfer and met his wife Alice Mary Glover at a golf club dance. She was also a golfing enthusiast and they fell in love. However, there was an obstacle in their way. He was Jewish and she was a Christian. Despite this, the Bloombergs decided they would never allow religion to come between them and were married in the Birkenhead Registry Office on 12 September 1922. As Simon had been disowned by his Jewish family for marrying a Gentile, none of them came to the wedding ceremony. Life for the newlyweds was one of dedication to His Majesty's Colonial Service with much travel and sacrifice. They would have five children: Bill; Marion (Marie); Norah (Binky); John Henry (Harry); and Eva. Norah would later compile a Bloomberg Family Tree documenting the family's travels, which has provided many of the details recorded in this brief biography.

> *"It was only later that I learnt that mum had promised dad she would take us to a safe place. I never realised then, that as half-Jews we would have been exterminated if Hitler had ever got to England."*

Norah describes how she and her siblings were sent to boarding school in Keswick while her parents and younger sister Eva were in Nairobi. "It was a traumatic experience for us, especially the little ones, but in those days, that was what one did. It was thought of as doing the best for your children. Harry was hardly eight years old and it knocked him. Unfortunately, he had ear problems and needed to have several operations. This resulted in Mum returning to the UK with Eva where she set up home for us kids, while dad was away serving King and Country."

According to Norah, Simon returned to England on leave in 1938 but had to go back to work in Kenya shortly before World War II broke out and the family wasn't reunited until 1942. She shares how her mother and siblings survived the war. "When the bombing started mum took us to live in a cottage in Wales halfway up a mountain, our only water was from a spring half a mile away and there was no school. After a while, we moved to a village where there was a junior school for Eva (but the lessons were in Welsh and foreigners weren't really welcome!) Marie and I were able to take a bus to Ruthin where we went to school. Harry won a scholarship to a public school in Canterbury, Kings and for a time was evacuated to Cornwall.

"It was only later that I learned that mum had promised dad she would take us to a safe place. I never realised then, that as half-Jews we would have faced the same fate as our European kinsfolk if Hitler had ever got to England. We lived like this for four years. Mum was courageous, she grew

Life After Belsen

all our own vegetables, kept us clothed and cheerful, often playing the piano and singing in the evening, when she wasn't knitting socks for the soldiers."

After completing a degree in forestry at Bangor, Bill joined the army and was sent to India where he served with the engineers. Harry also became a soldier and worked for MI5. Norah later went to Persia (Iran) where she was involved in outreaches to Jewish people in Tehran, before returning to England to work as a teacher.

Returning home to the UK on leave in 1942 Simon found himself on a leaking boat with no rudder, adrift in the icebergs of Antarctica. Fortuitously his life was preserved and the only damage was that when he opened his suitcases he found them full of seaweed.

Following Simon's time in Kenya, he expected to be promoted to head of Customs and Excise but his superior at the Colonial Office was known to be anti-Semitic and he was overlooked. Instead, he managed to get a position in Jamaica where he served until 1944. He held the position of controller general responsible for a staff of seven hundred people, a turnover of five million pounds, and was also a member of Jamaica's Legislative Council. It was in Jamaica that Simon played a fateful game of golf that would shape his future when his golfing partner suggested he work for the United Nations. He retired from the Colonial Office at fifty and joined UNRRA in May 1945, just after the liberation of

Simon Bloomberg

Belsen. During his first year at UNRRA, he worked as director of Polish and Ukrainian Camps in Germany, where he helped to resettle refugees from all over Europe. In June, 1946 his focus turned towards helping Jewish survivors of the Holocaust when he became UNRRA director of the Belsen DP Camp, (Hohne) – the first Jewish person in this position. It was considered that his appointment would help foster better relations between UNRRA and the eleven thousand Jewish DPs in the camp. Simon brought about many changes at Belsen including increased distribution of food and clothing amongst the DP community mostly made up of Holocaust survivors. These measures along with his tireless attempts to maintain stability in the camp are well documented.

"During the period, I was the UNRRA director at the Hohne DP camp (Bergen-Belsen) a great deal of my time was spent carefully explaining the British policy to the displaced persons in an endeavour to counter the anti-British sentiment that existed among certain elements because of the trouble in Palestine," Simon wrote in February 1947 in a letter found in the Wiener Library in London. "During the difficult time I was at Hohne, there was not a single demonstration against the authorities whereas before I arrived, there were several outbursts."

German historians, Angelika Konigseder and Juliane Wetzel wrote about his time at Belsen in their book, *Waiting For Hope*. (Published by Northwestern University Press)

Life After Belsen

"The situation improved further with a change of UNRRA directors in the Summer of 1946: on 8 July 1946 Simon Bloomberg replaced Wheatman. Bloomberg had been an officer in the British Colonial Service. He knew the official mind and could talk on equal terms with the military and civil authorities. There was soon a different atmosphere at Belsen. The change was manifested in concrete terms in the distribution of clothes and other goods in quantities previously unseen in the camp.

The newly appointed supply officer was soon a very popular person with the camp residents. Bloomberg identified so closely with the Belsen DPs that he resigned his position as UNRRA director of the camp in protest against the authorities' refusal to recognise the Jewish refugees from Eastern Europe as displaced persons and grant them rations. However, he continued to serve the interests of the survivors, for he was soon appointed field director for Europe of the Jewish Committee for Relief Abroad."

Norah also wrote about her father's time at Bergen-Belsen drawing from the many conversations they shared together.

"Dad led an international team handling the many problems at Belsen. There were over ten thousand people, mostly the only surviving member of their family, some of the children didn't have names, only numbers, and didn't know which country they belonged to.

"The British liberators first had to bury the dead before they could take care of the living. Inoculation programmes were introduced and new medical facilities provided, as well as schools. At home, we collected bags of clothing for the Holocaust survivors and sent them over from England.

"As time passed at Belsen it became a bustling centre with football teams, orchestras, and at one time they had enough dancers for a whole ballet company. Many of the people were highly skilled, specialists in every field including medicine. Finally, despite the official orders, 'We are full', dad refused to close the gates of the DP camp to a new avalanche of starving Jewish refugees and was forced to resign as a matter of principle."

Simon fought hard for the right of Jewish refugees from Eastern Europe to be allowed to enter Belsen and

Life After Belsen

resigned in protest when UNRRA ruled they did not consider them to be displaced persons or entitled to receive rations. However, he found a way to stay on at the camp by joining the Jewish Committee for Relief Abroad. In his new position, as European director of the Jewish Relief Unit, he was able to continue assisting the people of the camp.

Upon taking up this appointment, Simon addressed his team across Europe with these words, found in another document housed in the Wiener Library. "The difficulties of our stupendous task in Europe can only be overcome by the continued efforts and self-sacrifice which have characterised the work of the field personnel since the days of liberation. I am pleased to be associated with a unit whose reputation stands second to none among the voluntary societies operating throughout Europe. Without your cooperation any efforts of mine will be in vain. But, I feel sure you will accept me as a leader and a colleague in this great work of mercy for our unfortunate people, the remnant of Jewry in Germany and elsewhere." (28 May, 1947)

According to Waiting For Hope, the Jewish survivors called themselves 'the Sh'erit ha-Pletah', the Spared Remnant referred to in Ezra 9:14-15 and 2 Kings 19:30-31. It was these people that the Jewish Relief Unit cared for so earnestly in the camps until 1948 when the State of Israel was founded and the displaced Jews of Europe started moving slowly to their ancient homeland.

Simon Bloomberg

Finally, it was through Simon's work with the Jewish Relief Unit that he would help deal with the plight of the four thousand plus 'Exodus Jews' who were turned back from the shores of Israel. Tragically they were put back behind barbed wire in former concentration camps. He was there to assist with their unfortunate disembarkation and he later wrote about the appalling conditions they faced. But, no matter what, they refused to give up and kept the 'Exodus spirit' alive. As director for Europe, Simon also helped launch the Central British Fund Appeal in the interest of Jewish DPs and Jewish communities all over Europe, speaking in London where he described his experiences as Belsen camp director. The Jewish Committee for Relief Abroad honoured his work with a certificate signed by its chairman, Leonard Cohen. "Presented to Simon Bloomberg in recognition of devoted service in helping the survivors of Nazi persecution to rebuild their lives."

> *"There were over ten thousand people, mostly the only surviving member of their family, some of the children didn't have names, only numbers and didn't know which country they belonged to."*

Life After Belsen

A prolific writer, Simon kept diaries throughout his life, including a detailed account of his time in post-war Germany, in manuscript format. Originally entitled *Tales of the Survivors of Belsen and Other Camps in Europe*, his reams of faded typed pages form the basis of this book. Simon also wrote hundreds of letters to his wife, Alice. He would address the letters to her as "Alice my own love", or "my dearest wifey", and often sign off with "God bless you and keep you well, Yours ever, Simon." He would write about all sorts of things including his work and she would keep each letter as a historical record of all he accomplished. In one letter from Belsen, Simon wrote, "Despite the many difficulties things are moving very slowly in the right direction. My prayer is that the British Government sees its way clear to allow the Jewish DPs to go quickly. Reading the news these days is almost like reading the book of Exodus in the Old Testament. The British Government is like Pharaoh hardening his heart all over

> *"Despite the many difficulties things are moving very, very slowly in the right diretion. My only prayer is that the British Government sees their way clear to let the Jewish DPs go quickly."*

again. If at least one hundred thousand are allowed to go, ours are first on the priority list and then I can come home to you."

After three years of serving displaced persons, Simon returned to England where he was finally reunited with Alice and his children. Ever eager to chase the sun it wasn't long before the family moved again. Having been offered his old job back in Jamaica the Bloombergs soon set off for Kingston. Bill and Harry had already left home so it was just Simon and Alice and their three daughters. Marie enjoyed the social life at first but was disillusioned by the lack of job opportunities on the Caribbean island and went to work in Canada. Norah was quick to follow suit and Eva completed her schooling in Kingston.

Following in their father's footsteps, each of the Bloomberg children would embrace a life of public service in their own way. After the war Harry went off to study to become a vet at the Royal College in London and eventually settled in New Zealand in 1954. Bill heard Canada was offering free passages to unskilled workers so he kept quiet about his degree and went as a logger. Fortunately, a skilled forester was required and he was promoted to work on aerial surveys of forests. He later worked as the editor of a scientific journal and went back to study, gaining a PhD in tree diseases from Vancouver University.

Marie trained as a nurse at an orthopaedic hospital and worked with pioneers in the physical repair work on

Life After Belsen

pilots who had been disabled during the war. Later she went to London to study physiotherapy and then to Springfield, Ohio where she set up a pre-school programme for severely disabled children. Norah went to Bedford to train as a teacher and stayed in England. She led a long fruitful life and was involved in many community projects. She passed away in 2016 leaving a legacy of well-educated children.

Eva received a PhD degree from Bristol University and worked as a teacher of French and Spanish in London where she and her husband, Roger had three children. She remembers her father, who she always called 'Pop' as a caring, compassionate person who would give the shirt off his back. She tells how after World War II her father went to visit a surviving Jewish cousin in Holland, who had been left penniless by the war. Simon gave him his whole suitcase of clothes keeping only what was essential to be decent on his return to England. "That is the kind of man he was," she says.

Simon had a great sense of humour that would sustain him through the many challenges he faced. He would often laugh about the fact that some people thought he looked like Joseph Stalin and apparently, he was once dragged off the Queen Mary because he was mistaken for being the Communist dictator!

He invariably had something funny to say and would never be caught out. During his time in East Africa, he was taken aback when the Sultan of Zanzibar paid an unexpected evening call. Somewhat embarrassed, the African leader started making apologies... "Don't worry, I always dine in my pyjamas!" Simon exclaimed. He always had an answer and looked to see the funny side of life. (Eva still has an elaborate Indian carpet that the Sultan gave to her mother.) She also recalls how one of her father's sisters left him everything she had in her will, so in later life there was at least some reconciliation between Simon and his Jewish family. Although he wasn't overly religious, he still cared about Jewish traditions and she remembers how he declined to be a pallbearer at a friend's funeral. As a Cohen, he could not be near a dead body.

"Those who are left wait for the day when they can shake off the bloodstained dust of Germany from their feet and start a new life in a free land, far away from this land of dreadful memories, please God may it be soon."

Eva says many of Simon's team members during his UNRRA and Jewish Relief Unit days were single Jewish women. "They all wanted to marry him, joking that he didn't have a 'proper' wife because my mother wasn't Jewish! But that didn't concern him, he and my mother were so wrapped

Life After Belsen

up in each other. He was a genuine person and fun and everyone loved him."

She describes how her father was a popular figure who never thought himself as superior to others and would often stop to chat to passers-by. "Whenever we walked together in London, there was always someone who'd come up to us at Piccadilly Circus or elsewhere and say, 'Simon, how are you?'"

Eva remembers, with a chuckle, how they were once approached by a beggar in Jamaica. "Beg you tuppence," the man said. "You're a big, strong guy, why are you begging?" Simon replied, observing that it was probably because he was filthy and therefore couldn't get a job. "Beg you tuppence, for some soap" the beggar cleverly replied.

"These were the kind of fun conversations my father had with people because he never saw others as lower than himself," Eva observes. "I'm sure he was the same at Belsen, stopping to talk to the survivors. Eva also remembers how her father came back from his three years of serving displaced persons in Europe with an address book full of names of people he had helped to resettle in different countries as far away as South America. She recalls being sent a blouse as a gift from a grateful recipient of her father's benevolence in going the extra mile to assist the DPs.

The British establishment offered Simon a knighthood, but he wasn't someone who sought a title and he declined. He

Simon Bloomberg

did, however, agree to become a Commander of the British Empire. So, in 1951 at age fifty-seven, he was awarded a CBE. He was travelling back to the UK by ship at the time and received the news by telegram from the Governor of Jamaica, Hugh Foot (later Baron Caradon) "Delighted to inform you that his Majesty the King has awarded you CBE in birthday honours stop. Most sincere congratulations."

It was timely that this honour came just as Simon was leaving public service for good, crowing his achievements. He would miss the warm climate of Jamaica and wouldn't stay out of the sun for long. Neither would he miss an opportunity to help displaced people wherever needed. In 1956, he assisted Hungarian refugees in Vienna and in 1957 worked amongst Egyptian Refugees during the Suez Crisis.

With five children, one in Canada, one in the USA, one in New Zealand and two in England many of Simon's final years were spent visiting these countries. His beloved soulmate, Alice passed away in 1977 and he lived the remaining few years of his life with his daughter Eva and son-in-law Roger and their family in London. He died on 23 April 1981. On his deathbed, he called out for Alice. They had a wonderful relationship spanning fifty-four years of marriage and despite long periods of being apart.

Over and above his role in caring for Jewish DPs and his support of their right to go to Israel, Simon wanted to leave a legacy in the modern Jewish state and was acknowledged

Life After Belsen

for his philanthropy in supporting tertiary education in Israel.

He is survived by his only remaining child, Eva Spiers and her children, Alistair, James and Charlotte. Also by the children of Bill, Marie and Harry and many great-grandchildren. He will not be forgotten by his descendants or by those he helped. Thankfully he was able to assist many displaced persons and Holocaust survivors to make a new home in a place that offered them life after Belsen. For those that did not make it, in the words of Gettysburg, "these dead shall not have died in vain – that this nation, under God, shall have a new birth of freedom." Having arisen out of the ashes of the Holocaust, the State of Israel stands today as a bastion of hope and freedom for the Jewish People.

- **If you met Simon or heard about him,
  Eva would like to hear from you via email at
  lifeafterbelsen@simonbloomberg.com**

Visit www.simonbloomberg.com

Appendix

Simon Bloomberg's soldier's pay book for use on active service in World War 1 where he is listed as a signaller. His religion is given as Hebrew.

Life After Belsen

LETTER OF RESIGNATION

To: The Director, UNRRA Central HQ
From: The Director, UNRRA Team 806, Belsen
18th October 1946

It is now three months since I reported the presence of Jewish Refugees at Belsen. These people arrived here after 1 July 1946 and under Technical Instruction No 6 could not be registered as displaced persons. The camp committee estimates there are two thousand and among them are very old and infirm people and young children. Their state is pitiable and they are living on the charity of the displaced persons in the camp, from whose meagre rations they receive just enough to stay alive. Many have been reunited with relations they have been separated from for years.

These refugees are living in frightful conditions in the barracks vacated by the Poles, without regular food, little or no bedding and an understaffed Jewish Relief Unit to look after them. They have been informed they can obtain German rations if they register with the authorities and are dispersed among the German population but they refuse to throw themselves at the mercy of the bürgermeisters knowing full well they will be differentiated against.

The situation is so distressing I feel that as a UNRRA official I can no longer carry out this policy regarding infiltrees with which I am in total disagreement. I am anxious to remain in my post and stay until the end to help care for the people at Belsen, but unless there is a change in policy I regret I shall have to resign. – Simon Bloomberg.

This Records the Loyal and Valued Services of

SIMON BLOOMBERG

to the United Nations Relief and Rehabilitation Administration in its Great Work of Relieving the Suffering and Saving the Lives of the Victims of War in the Liberated Countries

Director General

Washington, D.C.
31 December 1946

Life After Belsen

To: Mr Simon Bloomberg, European Director
Jewish Relief Unit.
From: Mr Leonard Cohen, Chairman,
Jewish Committee for Relief Abroad

5 February 1948

Dear Mr Bloomberg,

I need not tell you how grieved we all are that the time has come that you are leaving us. Our regret is, fortunately, tempered by the knowledge that you have put the organisation onto a strong basis and have made arrangements for the work to be carried on.

The twelve months that you have been with us have been for me personally the most pleasant I have enjoyed with the committee. Difficulties which in the past caused me much worry have been quickly dispelled by your kind heart, clear head and sense of humour, a combination not frequently to be found. I shall miss your counsel greatly.

I am afraid I cannot express adequately how much the committee appreciates the fine service you have rendered. I know that for your part the knowledge that you have been able to bring some happiness to the unfortunate lot of your fellow Jews will be reward and thanks enough.

Yours sincerely, Leonard Cohen.

Simon Bloomberg

Germany Austria Italy Holland Greece N.Africa Egypt

JEWISH RELIEF UNIT

Presented to

Mr Simon Bloomberg

in recognition of devoted service

from 12 May 1947 to 23 Feb. 1948

in helping the survivors of Nazi

persecution to rebuild their lives

Leonard Cohen

Life After Belsen

Bricks Without Straw
A Lesson In Tenacity

An article about the 'Exodus Camps' by Simon Bloomberg of the Jewish Relief Unit
(The Jewish Echo, 6 February 1948)

Relief work is a strain upon the emotions. So much so, that the most harrowing scenes have little effect upon the case-hardened relief worker, who, like the punch-drunk boxer, fails to feel the blows. Occasionally, however, some extraordinary experience finds a vulnerable spot and the relief worker reacts like a normal individual.

It was such an experience that I encountered after I climbed up the three flights of stone steps into the attic of one of the barracks at Sengwarden, where the 'Exodus Jews' are incarcerated. Perhaps incarcerated is not the correct word to use because they are free to come and go, but to people without status or papers, freedom to move around is illusory. The checks and restrictions imposed by the Germans and the British military police are as effective as the barbed wire of a prison camp.

The attic running the whole length of the barrack room below was partitioned into little rooms, either by improvised wallboards or old blankets and each room used as a classroom with children receiving instruction in semi-darkness from teachers working without textbooks and until recently without blackboard or chalk.

Outside a blizzard was blowing and the dismal light

seeping through the fanlight windows made the scene more miserable than ever. To make things worse, the central heating was as bad as the light. Only the pen of a Dickens could do justice to such a scene, but despite all these drawbacks, the classes go on and the children are glad to learn.

The teachers are Jews themselves supervised by a teacher of the Jewish Agency, performing prodigious tasks under the most difficult conditions. The few wooden benches are overcrowded, school desks simply do not exist and teachers have to rely on their memories.

The school population numbers five hundred, so one can imagine the immensity of the task. Jews have throughout history oft-times been condemned to making bricks without straw and they have somehow succeeded. Here they are again making foundation stones, creating the material and training young Jews to help build their new homeland in Palestine. Only the strongest can work under such conditions of adversity and still carry on.

Why do these conditions exist and why can't they be altered immediately? The reasons are that the wheels of Government grind exceedingly slowly and in the case of the Jews in Germany, their support has fallen on the Jewish voluntary agencies of the British Zone. It may be indifference or ineptitude on the official side that fails to provide the necessities for the education of these young children. If only they were to receive similar facilities to those provided for German children, but unfortunately that is not the case. So, we go on in our fight against official complacency and at the same time send in everything we have to help these gallant teachers in their uphill struggle.

Life After Belsen

7th May, 1951

My dear Bloomberg,

I have seen your letter No. 3/6/77a/49 of the 2nd of May addressed to the Colonial Secretary about the progress and state of the work in your Department, and I most sincerely congratulate you on all you have done for Jamaica.

It is a matter of keen regret to me personally that I shall not have your experienced advice to rely upon in future, for I very well know how valuable your contribution has been and how much we need men of your outstanding ability in the Government Service of Jamaica in these difficult days.

You have earned the sincere respect of the public and the Service and on leaving Jamaica you have the satisfaction of having rendered public service of the utmost value.

I convey to you, on behalf of Jamaica, a message of deep gratitude and, on behalf of myself, every good wish for the future.

Yours sincerely,
Foot

Bloomberg Esq.,

Simon Bloomberg

```
RECEIVED----------JUNE 6, 1951          JS
DATED-------------JUNE 6TH
FROM--------------KINGSTON JCA      (WUC)
          FR
```

GRATEFUL IF YOU WOULD PASS FOLLOWING MESSAGE TO BLOOMBERG PASSENGER SS MEDIA FROM GOVERNOR OF JAMAICA DELIGHTED TO INFORM YOU THAT HIS MAJESTY THE KING HAS AWARDED YOU CBE IN BIRTHDAY HONOURS STOP I SEND YOU MOST SINCERE CONGRATULATIONS AND AM SURE THAT HONOUR WILL BE MOST POPULAR ONE AMONGST YOUR FRIENDS AND COLLEAGUES HERE

(SIGNED) GOVERNOR

Printed in Great Britain
by Amazon